Kibbutz

a memoir

Joseph Birchall

Although this is a work of non-fiction, the author has changed
most of the names.
Any virtuous characteristics or physical exquisiteness that you
feel may have been used, albeit unwittingly, to represent you,
you might possibly be right.
For all other less honourable and appealing characters,
I didn't mean you. Honest.

To my parents

ACKNOWLEDGMENTS

Apart from the physical act of sitting down and actually writing this book, it would not have been completed without the continuous, complete and constant support of Eileen. Your patience is ineffable, but truly appreciated. Thank you for your loving generosity, your generous love and for bringing me home.

Thanks to editor Brenda O'Hanlon who skillfully cropped, cut, and chopped away at sentences and whole paragraphs with such lexicographical dexterity and expertise. Thank you also for your continuing 'go for it' attitude and encouragement.

Thanks to Andrew Brown for his patience and talent in designing the cover.

Thank you to Kay, Shane, Brent, Maya and Gráinne for proofreading, and of course for their encouragement and feedback.

Special thanks to Shay, the first person to whom I had the courage to show the first draft. Your initial input and advice was not wasted.

Finally, thanks to the myriad of ex-volunteers, soldiers, children, members (and ex-members), chickens and everyone of Kibbutz Sederah (you know who you are!). You are my second home. See you down the Tea House soon...

'There are only two tragedies in life: one is not getting what one wants, and the other is getting it.'

Oscar Wilde

1

I had just turned twenty when I first visited the kibbutz; the year was 1990.

About my life up to that point, there's really not a whole lot to tell. I was brought up in Tallaght, a working-class area, which by the 1970s had become a major satellite town on the outskirts of Dublin. My grandparents had moved there in the 1930s, a time when Tallaght appeared as little more than a tiny, black dot on maps of the Greater Dublin area. By the mid-1980s, when I was a teenager, that tiny black drop had expanded and grown into a bulbous, ugly blotch. As I grew, so too did the town around me. Row upon row of houses spread out domino-like in all directions, unfettered by any geographical formation or aesthetic considerations. Architectural plans were photocopied and passed around to absentee developers. Trees were felled and vast green areas were concreted over. An expanse of box-like dwellings stretched outwards to the foot of the Dublin Mountains, and then tenaciously clambered up its leg. Infrastructure mainly consisted of roads designed to provide access to yet more houses, and it wasn't until years and years later that someone finally had the wisdom to shout 'STOP'.

I had, and still have, two wonderful parents who worked assiduously to make sure I wanted for nothing. Although I know they struggled at times and often went without – I never had to. I had, and still have, two brothers, whom I can call on today for anything and two caring sisters of immense generosity. When I was nineteen, I was more troubled than troublesome, and I longed to travel. I have often been asked why I left Ireland, and although I have given various half-hearted answers, I believe that I have just now stumbled upon the real truth – I was bored.

So much attention in books and films is devoted to the topic of the disadvantaged, the downtrodden and the deprived upbringing of children throughout the world, but very little attention is devoted to another deserving group – the disinterested, the impartial, the detached. I have no intention of redressing that balance here, but I do remember a constant feeling of apathy about my surroundings and an almost total disregard for my insipid peers. Perhaps I could have resolved everything by getting off my lazy arse and going rock climbing in the west of Ireland or maybe learning the guitar and joining a band, but I'm sure I would have viewed both options as lame and tame at the time. So, as usual, I overreacted and decided to leave the country.

A plan was hatched. I was due to finish my apprenticeship as a mechanic in late spring 1990, and I would then be free to set off on my travels. The previous year I had seen a documentary on BBC One about life on a kibbutz in Israel, and I can still vividly remember the images of sunshine, desert, trees and scantily-clad Swedish girls reaching out for ripe fruit. One of the German volunteers said that he had come to the kibbutz to 'get out of the rat race for a while', and I used to give that as my reason for going, whenever anyone cared to ask. More than twenty years later, I cringe to think of this excuse. A nineteen-year-old mechanic with neither a care nor want in the world complaining about the rat race. I was more of a hamster; the only running I ever took part in was on the Tallaght Bypass at five minutes to nine on my way to work, or on my way home at lunchtime to watch an episode of *Neighbours*. Rat race indeed.

In the continuous economic roller coaster that forms the very backbone of the Irish economy, we were very much in a downward spiral in the late 1980s, and so news of a young man heading abroad would hardly have caused a blip on anyone's radar. It was also the summer of Italia '90. A lot of strange people were doing a lot of strange things. The country was experiencing a football frenzy that culminated and climaxed in a quarterfinal playoff against Italy. On a Saturday night on 30 June, and after only thirty-eight minutes, Schillaci shattered our delusions of grandeur. That night, as people in pubs throughout Ireland drank and commiserated with one another on their bogusly perceived participation in the Irish team's achievements, my packed bags sat on my bed at home, waiting patiently. The following day, I left a hungover Ireland to pick up the pieces, and I was gone.

Before wandering my way into the land of milk and honey, I decided to stop off in France for the summer. My plan was to write, in my best possible French, to every small hotel along the Côte d'Azur, and then to choose the one I thought best, based on remuneration, its proximity to a beach and the chances of meeting as many loose French women as possible. Only one wrote back, so I chose that one. I was invited to work for two months, *juillet et août*, seven days a week with afternoons off; the sum of eight thousand francs would be paid at the end of my stay. With my Leaving Certificate maths, I worked out quite quickly that this equated to one thousand francs a week, or roughly one hundred Irish pounds. Both accommodation and meals would be included, and the use of the swimming pool for the entertainment of French girls would, of course, be permitted, but only in the afternoons. It wasn't until well into July that I realised there were in fact nine weeks in the two months, but given the complications of dividing eight into nine, I let it pass.

After my two months in France, I planned to travel around Europe for a while and then on to Israel, where I hoped to remain until Christmas, and then jet home, tanned and exotic, before setting off for Australia to work there for a year. Who was it that once asked, 'How do you make God laugh?', the reply to which is: 'Tell him your plans!'

All was going well in France, and I was having a wonderful time. The proprietor was a very large, hard-working, hard-faced but soft-hearted woman called Madame Aguillion. I had bought an oblong-shaped bottle of perfume for her in the Dublin Airport duty free shop as a gift, and she seemed pleased enough with this. Her husband, my namesake, was a benign and slender gentleman with a secretive yet sweet smile, and a penchant for olives, which he ate by the handful, spitting out the pips into his left hand. Every morning he would place a locally produced bottle of cabernet sauvignon just inside the door of the walk-in fridge in the kitchen and take sips from the bottle throughout the day – a habit, like our name, which we soon shared. Neither husband nor wife spoke a word of English. One evening, when I quizzed Madame Aguillion on popular culture, I discovered she had never heard of the Beatles, but had definitely heard of Elvis – *'le roi du rock 'n roll, n'est-ce pas?'*

The hotel, a three-star called *Hotel Saint Michel*, was small and was situated in the hills above the idiosyncratic French Riviera town of Villefranche-sur-Mer. It had about twenty rooms, which remained mostly vacant throughout the summer; a large clean swimming pool; a magnificent terrace, shaded by tall trees and wild plants, which provided respite from the Mediterranean sun in the afternoons and perfumed the air in the warm evenings; a long dining room with a magnificent two-foot high fireplace and, finally, the heart of the hotel, the kitchen, where Madame Aguillion would spend most of her time preparing, serving and then cleaning up after the three meals a day she provided for the guests.

It was the kitchen that I was most drawn to. For breakfast, the long baguettes taken from the freezer were chopped up diagonally and allowed to thaw; small yellow waves were shaved from chunky lumps of butter, like bars of gold, using a steel curler that required constant dipping into a cup of boiling water. The not-so-fresh baguettes from the previous day's breakfast were chopped into rounds and heated in the oven until they became brown and crispy; coffee, rich and sweet, was served in bowl-like cups that you would dip the buttered bread into. The simplicity and yet the extravagance of it all – *salade Nicoise*, *soupe de poissons*, *pain bagnat*, *pissaladière Nicoise*.

Dinner in Ireland usually meant someone slaving for hours to produce a pork chop, turnips and potatoes, and as delectable and nourishing as they were, the culinary surprises laid before me on that French oak table awakened taste buds in me that had lain dormant for years. And the speed. Who taught the Irish to boil cabbage, potatoes and all things good and green until every last vitamin and palatable pleasure was eliminated and we were left with limp reminders of their former vegetative selves? Who told us that a steak needed to be flipped over and over in the frying pan until cooked through, and until it became so chewy that it would form chewing gum-like lumps in your mouth?

Madame Aguillion would place a shallow pan of olive oil over a high heat. Two, three potatoes peeled and sliced, then into the pan. Lettuce, cleaned, dried and then thrown onto our plates, was followed by a little olive oil, salt and freshly ground pepper. The only pepper I'd previously seen was brown and powdery, like spicy dust that had been swept up from a Mexican's workshop floor. Three thin steaks, more olive oil on a fresh pan, over a high heat. On they go, count to *dix* and flip. *Pomme frites* out of the pan and onto the plates. Off come the steaks and *voilá* – dinner is served. Ten minutes at most. The aromas of freshness and opulence, the precision and efficiency of plates and pans, the taste of meat that cut and melted like butter, cold lettuce complementing the hot fries, olive oil combining with the blood of the rare steaks and all washed down with chilled red wine. Every meal was followed by baguettes and cheese: camembert, brie, roquefort, beaufort, and then fruit. Even the approach to eating fruit was different: cut and then placed in one's mouth with a knife, barely touching the fruit with one's hands. And then, of course, the inevitable espresso. Never once in France did I see anyone scoop a heaped spoon of instant coffee into a cup and add boiling water.

A retired couple from Paris, who owned an apartment in Nice and a boat in the marina, befriended me. They would spend the summer months in Villefranche-sur-Mer and abandon Nice to the tourists. Now that's chic. They owned a convertible Mercedes, and sometimes in the afternoons, we would drive up the coast towards Italy, past Eze in the hills, Cap-d'Ail and into Monaco, before turning around and heading home. We often stopped for coffee or to eat Italian ice cream, enjoying the celestial scene of white boats, blue seas and the golden sun from the comfort of our Mercedes leather seats. On one occasion they took me water skiing near Nice, where we pursued a ferry heading out to sea, weaving in and out between the giant waves that cascaded off the back of the ferry, with me hanging on for my life behind their speedboat.

One afternoon, in early August, while waiting in a barber's shop to have my hair cut, I read in the local newspaper, *Nice Matin*, about a man called Saddam Hussein, and how he was causing all sorts of commotion in the Middle East. His personal ambitions were to affect hundreds of thousands of lives, including my own. Although six months later, technically, he did try to kill me, in hindsight his actions proved to have a more positive than negative effect on my life. He and I shared the same birthday, 28 April, so I suppose it was for these reasons that I felt somewhat melancholic in 2006 when he was finally tried and hanged.

In late August, Kuwait was invaded, and there was trouble brewing in the Middle East. Ignoring my parents' justified apprehension, I set off for Tel Aviv; with eight thousand francs in my pocket I felt I could afford to be tenacious. I kissed Madame Aguillion and Joseph goodbye, and although our parting couldn't be described as grief-stricken, it was genuinely sombre. Madame unsuccessfully fought back tears, and when I hugged her goodbye, she smelt, for the first time, of the perfume I had bought her.

I have never been back to visit Villefranche-sur-Mer, but I still harbour a desire to sit on the terrace under the trees and dip buttered slices of baguette into soup bowls of coffee. The hotel is still there, but, sadly, Madame Aguillion and Joseph have since passed away.

I left Nice at the beginning of September on an overnight train to Rome. Just two months earlier, I had stepped off a plane and fallen into the metaphorical arms of Madame Aguillion; it was only now, as I was heading into the great unknown, that I felt for the first time that I had really left home. Growing up with two brothers and two sisters, there had always been the hustle and bustle of activity somewhere in the house. As I sat on the train, with the darkening foreign sky descending from the hills and enveloping me, I felt alone and I even had a sense of vulnerability.

After spending a couple of days sightseeing in Rome, I took another train to Brindisi on the east coast of Italy, and from there a ferry to the Greek capital before finally making my way to Athens airport where I bought a ticket to Tel Aviv. Why I didn't just go to Marseille and fly directly I'll never know. To retrace one's physical steps requires quite a bit of effort, but to decipher the thoughts and motivations that were going on in one's head twenty years ago can be an exercise in futility.

My brother had spent a year in Germany working in an American airbase in 1988, and when he returned to Ireland he brought back with him a US Army kit bag. It was this that I was now using as my luggage, and it was so stuffed with clothes that it looked like a boxer's punching bag. Again, why I would burden myself with such a cumbersome piece of luggage that afforded me only a small chance of extracting exactly what I was searching for, is completely beyond me. Surely I must have seen backpacks and was aware of the invention of pockets?

It was a night flight over the Aegean Sea and down into the Mediterranean that carried me safely to Tel Aviv. The plane was mostly full of young people. With the prospect of a war in the Middle East looming, I was glad to realise that I wasn't the only person ignoring international media reports. Some of the people on the plane spoke a language I'd never heard before, and although it was Germanic in tone, it was softer, as if the sharp edges of German words had been filed down on both sides. It had the 'ch' sound as in the Scottish word 'loch'. They spoke it loudly with great emphasis but not ostentatiously; it was delivered with pride.

Almost everyone clapped as the wheels touched down, and I later saw one or two of the group kissing the ground when they disembarked from the plane. I thought of how Pope John Paul II had done exactly the same when he landed in Ireland ten years previously. I had barely touched the apparently sacred soil of Israel, and already metaphorical religious connotations and pious paradigms were raining down upon me from the heavens.

I feel it an appropriate time to pause a moment and offer a slight caveat and confession (pun intended) that I would not regard myself as a fully paid-up member of the Catholic Church. I believe my subscription expired sometime in my late teens, and I haven't as yet renewed it. Nonetheless, I do understand the sensitivity of these matters, especially in a country embedded in, or arguably blighted by, a hallowed homage and is imbued with such spiritual significance for the three major religions of the area – Judaism, Islam and Christianity. Therefore, I will endeavour throughout my ramblings, both verbal and pedestrian, to think of eggshells and wear the lightest of footwear; perhaps even sandals.

For thousands of years, disparate domains of dictatorships and democracies have fought to acquire a piece of this beautiful and beatified land. And yet despite all ethereal guarantees, I doubt that one could have, at any time in the past, conjured up enough milk in Israel to fill a small glass, let alone enough honey to spread on a piece of toast, unleavened or not. But, as for tears and blood, the place has been awash with the stuff ever since God looked down and said, 'Let there be light.' I doubt if Moses would have been so easily won over with the phrase, 'A land of blood and tears'. A little bit of 'bigging it up' from God, I assume. Anyway, this is not a political treatise, and besides, there are already a myriad of wonderfully biased books written by many wonderfully biased writers who either confirm or contradict any number of particular, or indeed peculiar, persuasions on the subject.

Although it was getting late in the evening when I stepped into the Israeli air, the heat hit me like a charging bull. My scant knowledge of Tel Aviv was such that the name had always been synonymous with bombs and war, similar in reputation to the Beirut of the 1970s. Happily, I arrived to find a city that was not dissimilar – in terms of first appearances at any rate – to any modern European city on a Saturday night. I found a taxi and headed for a hotel. Frugality was uppermost in my mind, as I had already ploughed through my small mountain of cash on my journey thus far. I still had to survive a full four months before heading home in December. I stayed in a small hotel near the beach in a room overlooking a water fountain that played host to a crowd of late-night drinkers, spontaneous singers and loud debaters.

Saturday, or Shabbat, is the Jewish day of rest, and Sunday is the first working day of the week. So, when I left the hotel the following morning, I found myself in a fully functioning, vibrating and noisy city. Fearing for the safety of my worldly possessions, I took the five-feet tall green punching bag with me. Turning the corner, perhaps two hundred metres from the hotel, I stopped – exhausted. I could feel the straps of the bag creating a channel between my right collarbone and my shoulder blade, and I felt my head and face turning a bright red. Sweat seemed to be oozing profusely from every pore of my skin. The pretty receptionist had given me a small street map, on which she had graciously added the ever coveted 'X', indicating the address of the volunteers' office where I needed to sign the appropriate papers and be assigned to a particular kibbutz. She assured me that the office was within walking distance; but everywhere is within walking distance if one has the time.

I checked the map and switched the bag from my right to my left shoulder. I must have looked a sight. The street signs were in Hebrew and English, and I estimated that it would take me about thirty minutes to get there. I contemplated being extravagant and hailing a taxi, but I was sure I'd get ripped off. So, at the risk of dehydration at best and heat stroke at worst, I sauntered on.

I passed the street signs of Ben Yehuda, Frishman, Shalom Aleichem, until turning onto Dizengoff. Tree-lined and extremely cosmopolitan, it contrasted sharply with the antiquated alleyways that I'd been working my way through. It had numerous cafes; tables and chairs spilled out onto the path where they were fenced off like little gardens. Parasols sprouted like prodigious plants, casting a gratifying shade over the cafes' patrons. I briefly considered stopping to sit and sip on something cold, but I was anxious to find the office and get to my assigned kibbutz before evening. As I trudged along, I remembered a video by David Bowie called *Let's Dance*. It featured an Aboriginal man pulling a heavy piece of machinery through the streets of some metropolis. I could recall the exertion on his face, and I started singing the song quietly to myself like a mantra, over and over. I switched my bag from one shoulder to another, but each time I did, it seemed to get bigger and heavier as my feet slowly melted into the scorching concrete footpath.

The volunteers' office consisted of two small rooms on the second floor of a building off King George Street. I had filled out a few rudimentary forms before leaving Ireland, and I handed these to the woman while taking my seat in front of her. She showed as much interest in the forms as she did in her job, or as she did in me for that matter. Her demeanour expressed so much ennui and apathy that I was positive she had practised it for hours in front of a mirror at home. I'm quite certain that if she had smiled, the building would have shaken slightly.

She was, albeit unwittingly, about to make a decision that would affect the rest of my life.

As I waited, obediently, I read through a small pamphlet that explained the comings and goings of your average run-of-the-mill kibbutz, its *modus operandi* and the initial reasons for its inception.

The kibbutz movement was established in the early twentieth century by Jews fleeing a series of pogroms in their native Russia. Kibbutzim (its plural name) are predominantly agriculturally-based communities with a socialist and Zionist ethos. The agricultural land in the territory known as Palestine in the early twentieth century was quite impotent and feeble. Worse, recently arrived Jewish immigrants often found themselves under physical attack from the indigenous Bedouin Arabs – an ancient nomadic and mostly desert-dwelling people. Seeking safety in numbers, the immigrants amalgamated their skills, their labour and their dreams, and set up the first kibbutz just south of the Sea of Galilee. Due to the extremely harsh climate, the work was almost unbearably difficult and arduous; many immigrants felt the labour involved wasn't worth the effort and left, but a few stuck it out, overcoming what seemed like insurmountable obstacles. By dint of sheer toil and effort, they miraculously breathed life into the barren soil and transformed it from an arid brown to a flourishing green. Soon, other kibbutzim began popping up, and today they number over two hundred and fifty. The number of residents in the kibbutzim varies, but most have between two hundred and five hundred adult members known as kibbutzniks. Earnings are divided up and shared according to individual needs. A doctor with one child will receive a smaller allowance than a factory worker with three children. 'From each according to his ability, to each according to his needs,' as Karl Marx wrote.

Most kibbutzim have communal swimming pools, large dining halls, sport centres and crèches for the children. One's laundry is washed, ironed and folded, one's food is cooked, and one's dishes are cleaned. Then throw in a resident doctor and nurse, a dentist who visits regularly and medical care for any health problem that may arise at any age. And it's all-inclusive. Not a shekel. Just do your work and be an effective and congenial kibbutznik, and Utopia shall be yours. Although from my experience, even efficiency and congeniality aren't imperative. Unfortunately, Jean-Paul Sartre informed us that, 'hell is other people,' and therein lies the rub.

'What part Israel you want to go?' she suddenly asked me, her heavy accent reverberating through the meagre office where we sat.

Since I had planned on going home in December, I thought it best to choose the south, the Negev desert; my thinking being that I would catch as much of the sun as possible before the winter set in. I would return home triumphantly and with a tan in time for Christmas. I may also have fancied my chances of transforming into a latter-day Irish Lawrence of Arabia in a few short months, although I'd probably be called Larry, and instead of a camel, the ship of the desert, I'd be given a donkey. Secretly, at home in Dublin, I had watched the rock opera *Jesus Christ Superstar* countless times; it had been shot in the Negev. Above all, I had, and still have, an inexplicable infatuation for the desert.

'I was thinking,' I timidly suggested. 'I was thinking of the south. The Negev or somewhere...'

'Why?' she interrupted me, dabbing her forehead with a small, white cloth, while strenuously avoiding eye contact with me. 'It's not hot enough for you here?'

I thought her question rhetorical so didn't answer; in the ensuing silence the din of city traffic seeped through the closed window. I turned to look out, but the dusty white shutters blocked any view. Engines revved and cars braked; it was a similar sound to what I'd hear in Dublin, but with a slight difference. The noise had an assertiveness that was just short of aggression; an intensity that was slightly shy of overzealousness; a familiarity that was somehow alien to me. The same but – well, not the same. This was a theme I was to see play out over and over during my time in Israel – take nothing for granted; discard all assumptions; when in doubt, stay in doubt.

When I turned back to her, her face was still pointed downwards at the table, but her eyes were now directed upwards, observing me. A lethargic smile hung heavily on her face. Christ, I thought. This is her in a good mood!

'You know who was David Ben-Gurion?' she asked.

'Em, was he a prophet?'

She sat up in her chair and looked at me incredulously. Obviously, this was not the right answer. She took a green, postcard-sized form from a drawer in the desk, and with great decisiveness, filled it up in what I assumed was Hebrew and then handed it to me. I'm not sure if she thought me impertinent or just stupid. I took the form and looked at it. There was only one word written on it in English: Sederah. In my thick Irish accent I pronounced the name of the kibbutz, my new home. She sighed heavily at my attempt, but clearly didn't regard me as impertinent any more.

'You will be perfect for this kibbutz,' she told me and went back to her paperwork.

I sat there for a few seconds looking at the card and then at her, and then back at the card. 'But how do I...?' I asked her.

She looked back at me, almost surprised that I was still there. Standing up, she went to a filing cabinet, searched through some files and pulled out a white A4 page. She handed it to me.

'Take,' she instructed. I took.

On it was information about Kibbutz Sederah, a few paragraphs about its history and how it could be reached by car, bus and, surprisingly, airplane. Since I had neither car nor plane, I began to read the bus transport instructions. She had returned to her chair and was glaring at me.

'*Shalom*,' she said. Shalom is a beautiful word that literally means 'peace' but is used more commonly as a greeting to say 'hello' or 'goodbye'. Its amicable ambiguity is open to interpretation, but I knew what she really meant by it – 'Now, piss off.'

With the green paperwork in one hand and the green punching bag over my shoulder, I headed back out into the searing hot city streets.

2

Israel is a land of contrasts and contradictions: from dusty arid deserts in the south to lush agricultural fields in the north; from the ski resort on Mount Hermon in the Golan Heights to the lowest point on Earth at the Dead Sea; from the sophisticated metropolis of Tel Aviv to the archaic traditions and lifestyle of the nomadic tribes in the Negev. Even its people are diverse. In the blue corner we have peace-loving, meditating and mediating, tree-hugging, free-thinking, flower-wearing, bohemian hippies and in the red corner we have cantankerous, polemic, spiteful, fanatical, Arab-loathing pugnacious warmongers. All this in a country the size of Wales and with a population of only seven and a half million people.

I considered these contrasts as I made my way on foot to the main Tel Aviv bus station. Modernity side by side with antiquity. Men in Armani suits on mobile phones cruising past Orthodox Jews in traditional black garb. Beautiful girls in tight denims, belly tops and high-heels striding by no-less-attractive girls wearing multi-coloured, pyjama-like clothes with no makeup and unkempt hair. And soldiers. Lots of soldiers. Men and women, or rather boys and girls, wearing green uniforms; many of the shirts and trousers ill-fitting and loose on the skinny bodies they covered; M16s slung over their shoulders in the style of a sports bag being carried home from the gym.

After another two blocks, I rounded the corner of a narrow street and turned into a large space and there was the bus station – a maelstrom of noise, colour and activity. Small blue and white city buses whizzed around the station, dropping off passengers to the larger red provincial buses. All around the outside of the station, stallholders were selling a myriad of goods ranging from television sets to batteries, and enough food to feed a small army, which was just as well as a small army seemed to be taking up most of the available space in the station. Vendors called out their promotional spiel in Hebrew, but switched to English as I walked by.

'Hey, you want falafel?'

'You want kebab, my friend?'

'Hey shalom. You eat here. It's very good.'

Smoke rose from the different meats being cooked, sometimes obscuring the vendors themselves. As it wafted out onto the path, it carried smells that set my mouth drooling and my eyes watering. I was suddenly very hungry but wanted to first buy a ticket for my bus, the number 370, to a town called Beersheba, about one hundred kilometres south of Tel Aviv. From there, I was to take another bus, a number 60, to Kibbutz Sederah. That's what the information sheet said anyway, and what position was I in to argue? As I queued for my ticket, I thought the station had a very African feel to it; heat and soldiers and with a kind of grubby, working disorder to the place. Without wishing to state the obvious, it was the most foreign country I'd ever visited. I bought my ticket from the surly cashier using the shekels that I'd exchanged from French francs at a *bureau de change*. She threw my ticket and change at me without once looking in my direction.

'Thank you,' I said. 'I think I met your sister earlier.'

'*Ma?*' (what?) she asked.

The next number 370 bus was due to leave in forty minutes, which gave me plenty of time to get something to eat. I was determined to try something new, and although the idea of kebab meat was appealing, I was conscious of the risk of eating something dodgy, and then having to sit on a bus for two hours. From the nearest vendor I ordered falafel and salad in pita bread. I went back and waited for my bus at a long wooden bench where four or five people were already seated. I took out the sheet that the volunteers' office had given me and read about the history of the kibbutz.

Apparently, David Ben-Gurion was not a desert-dwelling prophet from Deuteronomy; he was, in fact, one of the founders of modern Israel and its first Prime Minister. When he retired from office, he moved to Kibbutz Sederah and lived there until his death in 1973. I wondered if that meant she had sent me to work in a retirement home. Instead of picking bananas from tall, luscious trees with Swedish girls sporting similar attributes, would I instead be emptying bedpans and handing out multi-coloured pills to ninety-year-olds? I could picture the woman back in the volunteers' office cackling with laughter, her feet up on her desk, telling her colleagues what she'd done that morning, as they all stood around, holding their sides and howling at the hilarity of it all.

I wanted to ask someone in the queue beside me if anyone had heard of this retirement village in the middle of the desert. To my right, an old woman was eating some kind of seeds from a half-full, brown paper bag on her lap. I thought her perhaps a little mad, as she placed each seed into her mouth and then bit down on it, the seed making a cracking sound before she spat it out again into her other hand. I figured she was being litter-conscious until she emptied the contents of her fist onto the ground, where a small mound of discarded seed shells was growing ever larger by the minute. Beside her sat an Orthodox Jew dressed in a black suit with a large black hat; a white shirt, buttoned at the top; thick, black-rimmed glasses. A busy and untidy brown beard and two, almost twelve-inch curls flowed down either side of his face, dangling like the hairy legs of some creature hidden under his hat. He looked like most men of God, based on my personal experience: harsh, acerbic, and best left alone.

To my left, three soldiers chatted and smoked regular-looking cigarettes extracted from packets made of green paper and featuring a brand name I'd never seen before. Unusually for me, I hadn't had a cigarette since I'd left Athens the day before. I wondered if their cigarettes were produced in special packaging designed for soldiers – in a green camouflage, like their uniforms. On the other hand, where was all the vegetation and greenery that they were supposed to blend in with? Thus far, all I'd seen was grey, city buildings, and I was heading for, I presumed, a brown desert. Back on Dissengorf Street, I had seen a bunch of soldiers in beige-coloured uniforms. Perhaps, I thought, they were desert soldiers, and their light-coloured uniforms were designed to blend in with the sand there. I was sure one of my fellow bus passengers would know something about this retirement home. The strains of Israeli folk music emanated feebly from the bus station public address system, but it sounded more Arabic than Jewish to me, not that I could absolutely distinguish the difference. Every now and again they would play some obscure hit song in English from the 1970s or 1980s. I don't know what I expected though: twenty-four hours of *Hava Nagila* perhaps.

I realised that a sense of apprehension had overtaken me since earlier that morning, and had been increasing steadily, in tandem with the rise in the temperature. Without me noticing, the exoticness of my journey had changed from a feeling of excitement and optimism to one of trepidation and doubt. Whereas previously the idea of travelling alone had made me feel independent and autonomous, now I just felt, well, alone.

As I sat there determined to shake off that feeling and regain a sense of adventure, a fellow Dubliner came to my rescue. The enigmatic and eminent, although more eminent than enigmatic back then, Sinead O'Connor turned up on the public address system, and sang to me. And not just any song, but 'Nothing Compares to You.' It had been a massive hit in the six months before I had left Ireland; not having heard it for some time was like meeting an old friend who cheered you up. Her voice sounded tinny and metallic on the bus station's cheap speakers, but by the time the song was over, I felt far more sanguine and far less isolated. How perilous and threatening could a country really be if it played bald-headed Irish women crying on videos on MTV?

The temperature still seemed to continue rising as the day went on; the metal canopy above me barely prevented the sun from directly incinerating the hairs on my head and arms. I drank the last of the now tepid water from my plastic bottle and gazed over at the stall where I could buy more water for the two-hour journey that lay ahead. There were now about twenty people waiting behind me in the queue, and I didn't want to lose my place. Maybe the soldiers would guard my bags, and I could run over to the stall unhindered. Soldiers are like cops, right? You can trust them. Anyway, somebody somewhere must trust them enough to allow them saunter around with semi-automatic rifles. But I left it too late to ask: the bus pulled up quickly at the end of our bench, the side door already open.

Just then, an incredible thing happened. I had spent over twenty minutes in the queue, and there were about five people in front of me. As the bus pulled in, I bent down to put the information sheet away and to pick up my green kit bag. I must have had my head down for ten seconds or less. By the time I straightened myself up, most of the people who had been behind me in the queue were now standing in front of me. Even the soldiers I had considered entrusting with my worldly possessions only moments before almost knocked me down in their dash to get on the bus. I turned to see them battling with the old lady, her neat mound of discarded seeds now laid scattered all over the ground. She, in turn, was elbowing one of the soldiers slyly in the ribs, a devious move that would have won praise from an All Blacks scrum-half. It was quite literally a stampede. Could this possibly be the last bus out of Tel Aviv today? Was Beersheba such an amazing town that these people just couldn't wait to get there?

The luggage doors on the side of the bus were opened by soldiers who fired in their kit bags and boarded the bus without bothering to come back around and queue up with the rest of us. I thought of all the years I had been instructed to get in line and wait my turn by older, more patient people. It seemed to me that thousands of years of civilisation and advancements in culture and technology meant nothing when it came to finding an empty seat on a bus in Tel Aviv. There was nothing I could do but be carried along in a wave of bodies until I was swept up to face the driver. I handed my ticket to him.

'*T'sim et ha teek lemata,*' he said, gesticulating with his arms.

I stared blankly at him and looked at my ticket.

'Beersheba,' I said meekly.

'*Ha teek lemata*,' he practically shouted at me. I was all too aware of the side arm flapping on his belt as he pointed his finger at me. It was the first time an armed man had ever shouted at me, so I was quite keen to obey. Just then, the man standing behind me leaned in.

'He says to put your bag under the bus,' he told me.

'Under the bus?' I asked. 'Why would I put my bag under... oh, I see.'

Turning around, I tried to descend the steps, much to everyone's annoyance, as they were obliged to shuffle off the bus backwards in order to allow me and my bag to get through. I managed to shove it in with the other bags; it didn't look at all dissimilar to the army bags that were already there. I climbed the steps again – the last person to board the bus.

I flopped into the only vacant seat I could see – one shared with another soldier, and he was already asleep. As the bus door closed, I suddenly felt the effect of the cold air conditioning wafting over me. The driver confidently reversed out of the bay, and we roared through the streets of Tel Aviv, the bus stopping on a few occasions in the suburbs to pick up more people. More and more people got on, encouraged by aggressive barks from the driver for everyone else to move back, or at least I assumed that's what he was saying. Soon, the aisle was packed with people standing, but the driver seemed happy to continue stopping to pick up more. Eventually, it was the waiting passengers themselves who decided not to board the bus. This Beersheba place must be the Disneyland of Israel, I thought.

We made our way to the outskirts of Tel Aviv, high-rise concrete and glass giving way to fields of vegetation and grass. All the while, the music played from the driver's radio, and on the hour every hour he turned up the volume so that everyone could listen to the news. Beside me, the soldier's head lobbed from side to side, his face and open mouth pointing to the floor. As we left the city behind us, he began to snore lightly, which I found a little annoying, but honestly not that annoying when compared with the black-barrelled tip of his M16 that jabbed my ribs every time the bus swayed to the right. After about the tenth time this occurred, I courageously nudged him awake. He turned his head languidly to me, barely opening his eyes. I pointed to his gun and to my ribs, being very careful not to touch the gun. He hoisted it up over his head, propped it up against the window, leaned his head against the rifle and promptly fell back asleep.

The gentle rocking of the bus had an hypnotic effect on me, and the glaring sun outside made my eyes feel heavy. I soon nodded off, I'm not sure for how long, and when I opened my eyes it was as if we had driven into another country. For several moments I had no idea where I was. Just before I nodded off, we were driving past occasional buildings and streetlights, busy junctions and sporadic sets of traffic lights. Now, I could only see hills of rock and sand in various shades of brown stretching out as far as the eye could see.

The desert was not as I had imagined it. No rolling sand dunes like in *Lawrence of Arabia*, or the old French Foreign Legion films that I had seen. There were no undulating hills of smooth, soft golden sand dotted with palm tree-fenced oases. This was a grubbier landscape, harsh and jagged, like the blunted edge of a knife, and with spiky and bare vegetation littered about. The ground was scattered with rocks and stones, the hills stained in various tones that ranged from beige to brown to black. In sharp contrast to this dusty and gritty panorama I could see a glorious and ethereal sky uninhabited by clouds of any kind. It was as if the very land itself had had its green and luscious skin ripped from its body, and was now exposed and abandoned, underneath an unforgiving and garish sun.

I fell in love with it immediately. I have no idea why. As usual, love provided neither excuse nor explanation but there it was; a sense of homecoming, an adoration, a quickening of the pulse – I breathed in deeply.

A scattering of houses and buildings began to appear along the roadside. I leaned out of my seat and saw that we were approaching a built-up area. I looked at my watch: it was almost noon, so I knew that this must be Beersheba. The bus was only half full now, so the chances of this being Disneyland were slim. As we drove closer to the centre, the buildings appeared older, but in every other way it looked like an average-sized modern city. I knew from the information leaflet that the kibbutz was a further forty five minutes' journey: I liked the idea of not living too far from civilisation, or at least not too far from whatever form of civilisation this town had to offer.

As I got off the bus, I said thank you to the driver, but he ignored me. It wasn't until I had removed my bag from the luggage compartment and was walking towards the sign marked 'Information' that I realised the air temperature seemed to have doubled. My bag also seemed to have doubled in weight, and my pulse was quickening. Near the 'Information' sign was a stall selling food and drinks.

'You want falafel, my friend?'

'Water please.'

'I have kebab.'

'No, thanks. Just water.'

'You want Coca-Cola?'

'Do you have any water?'

Without saying another word, he reached back and took out a small bottle of water from the red, Coca-Cola fridge behind him.

'Five shekel,' he said, keeping the bottle out of my reach until I handed over the money. I had no idea whether five shekels was the equivalent of five pence or five pounds, but I handed it to him nonetheless, and he gave me the bottle. The water quenched the burning in my throat, and I honestly thought I heard a hissing sound. There may well have been steam coming out of my ears for all I knew.

Once again, I was keen to get to the kibbutz before it got too late in the afternoon, or before I melted – whichever came first. The 'Information' guy told me to take a number 60 bus;

that there'd be one leaving soon. I bought a ticket and joined the queue, which was already quite long. I had a fair idea that my actual place in the queue was inconsequential. I wandered over to the side of the waiting area so that I could stick my bag in the luggage compartment: I was determined to keep the number of armed men shouting at me down to single digits, at least on my first day.

The bus that pulled in was similar to the previous one I'd just been on except that the driver seemed more amiable and was unarmed.

'Kibbutz Sederah?'

'*Ken*' (yes).

Ken? Who's Ken? I thought.

'*Ken*,' he said again and pointed towards the back of the bus.

I looked down the aisle for this Ken. Was Ken going to tell me where to get off the bus? Was the driver's name Ken?

'Thanks.'

'*Ken, ken*,' he replied, and I moved into a seat not too far from the driver, hoping that Ken could see where I was.

The seat was empty, and I slid over to the window. I had left France almost a week ago, and was now less than an hour away from my final destination and my new home for the next four months. As the driver closed the door and reversed out of the bay, I thought of my home in Dublin; something I hadn't done in a while.

If I were at home in Dublin now, on a Sunday afternoon, I'd probably be recuperating from a Saturday night of binge drinking and chain smoking and a bellyful of late-night fast food. The sky would be grey with the possibility of rain, and my head would be sore with the possibility of a migraine. Saturday night's antics, along with a large portion of my wages, would, by now, be a blur. My mother would make a roast chicken dinner at three o'clock, which I would thanklessly consume before either venturing out or retreating back to bed with a book, and then the evening would quickly pass marked by an ever-increasing foreboding of Monday morning.

But here I was instead – in a foreign land among foreign people. Unlike the certainty that characterised my existence in Ireland, I had no idea what the next few months might entail. Every day would be unrehearsed and impromptu and every moment born out of a curiosity for something alien and unexpected – not relived and rehashed on a weekly basis, as my life had been up to that point. I realised that this was why I had left Ireland, and that this was the driving force behind my decision to come to this place, to any place – to explore the exotic, to travel this phenomenal world of ours, and above all, to cast aside the banality of my old life. To boldly go where no man, or at least no one I knew, had gone before. We drove out of the bus station, my apprehension having turned once again to anticipation.

By the time we passed the first junction, the drab, urban landscape had given way to desert. The road signage was written in three languages: Hebrew at the top, then Arabic, and English at the bottom. The further south we travelled, the less vegetation could be seen. I didn't have a map, but I knew that I was going south because I could recall a map of the Holy Land from my schooldays, in which Israel was divided up into various coloured sections. Of course, because I studied the map in religion class, the map related to the time of Jesus and featured place names such as Judea and Samaria. I felt though, as if I was on a bus into the unknown. I had seen that two-minute clip on television of the basics of a kibbutz from a volunteer's point of view, but I had no real idea of what it would actually involve.

The driver kept the radio on low and the air conditioning up high, as I gazed at the arid hills under a punishing sun. A Bedouin Arab, who smelt of campfire smoke as he walked down the aisle past me, got off at a bus stop that could only be described as in the middle of nowhere. As the bus pulled away, I turned to see where he was now standing. I looked at the horizon for miles in every direction, but could see nothing. The bus hummed along the road, swaying contentedly from side to side, before coming to a gentle, rolling stop. I have had the pleasure of travelling with Dublin Bus on many occasions, and instantly recognised the fact that we were now, unquestionably, all sitting in a vehicle that had broken down. With the air conditioning now turned off, the atmosphere quickly became thick and stuffy. I could feel my face becoming a little flushed and was glad when the driver, after one or two attempts to restart the bus, opened the doors. Some passengers mumbled and moaned, and with heavy, sullen footsteps ventured outside to further mumble and moan, and light each other's cigarettes in complaining camaraderie.

I suddenly remembered that I too was a smoker and decided to join them. As I got up from my seat, the driver made a short announcement, but he may very well have told us not to wander off too far as we would all be dead soon and it would be more difficult to round up the corpses, as I naturally didn't understand a word he said. I stepped off the bus, placing a cigarette in my mouth at the same time. As I went to light it, I could feel the heat radiating from the engine burning the skin on my face, so I walked on a little further. I tried to light my cigarette again, but the engine's overworked pistons, or maybe it was the body of the bus itself, gave off such an intense heat that I had to move quite a distance away. Standing at the side of the road, with my cigarette in one hand and my lighter in the other and at least thirty feet away from the bus and the driver, who still sat inanely pushing buttons on the dash, I quickly came to the conclusion that the offending and almost nauseating heat had nothing whatsoever to do with the bus or its engine.

My pulse was quickening; I inhaled through my mouth to get some oxygen into my body, but the air itself seemed parched, and I felt it scorching the back of my throat as I swallowed. I touched the top of my head and could feel heat rising from my hair. I needed to squint to stop the glare that reflected off everything around me.

A car drove by, the rush of air it stirred up pushing me backwards and creating no cooling effect whatsoever – more of a hair dryer effect. I looked at my watch and saw that it was just after one o'clock. The mad dogs and Englishmen quote of Noël Coward came to mind as I put away my cigarette and moved into the shade of the bus. I was impressed when, twenty minutes later, another bus arrived and we cheerfully made our transfer.

Finally there it was – a road sign with the name Kibbutz Sederah. My sigh of relief was quickly replaced with uncertainty as I realised that I had not been given a contact name or phone number.

'Thanks, Ken,' I said to the driver, as I descended the steps.

'*Ken, ken,*' he replied.

I suddenly realised just how isolated and small a community this place was. The perimeter fencing was completely surrounded by a hostile landscape. On a map of the world, Israel is little more than a tiny dot and on that dot is another pin-sized dot marking the spot where I now stood. I had made an insignificant step off a bus, but it was one that would have Neil Armstrongesque significance for the rest of my life.

I looked at my watch; it was nearly two o'clock. I checked the date and saw that it was 9 September 1990. My watch read 9-9-90. A good omen, I thought as I walked towards the main building.

3

A long, slender driveway that was lined with tall palm trees on either side, led to a spacious car park. As the door of the bus closed, the driver did a U-turn and took off with a roar of his engine back towards the main road, leaving in the wake of silence, a trail of dust and fumes that hung in the still air. I could see a signpost with at least ten signs on it, each one pointing in one of only two directions, displaying names such as 'The Factory', 'Chicken House Office', 'The Garage', 'Dining Room'. There was no reference to 'Irish volunteers who had just got off a bus from Beersheba', so I hoisted up my bag and wandered in the direction of the dining room.

From the opposite direction, a middle-aged woman passed me, cycling energetically. She must have observed my bewildered expression because she slowed as she approached me.

'*Shalom*,' she said, smiling.

'*Shalom*,' I replied, almost unaware that I had spoken my first Hebrew word. It left a funny aftertaste in my mouth, like sampling a food I had never eaten before.

'Do you need any help?' she said, switching to English. I'd obviously made a complete mess of even that one-syllable word.

'I'm afraid I'm a little lost,' I told her.

'Who are you looking for?'

'The volunteers' office sent me here,' I explained, almost apologetically.

'Oh, okay,' she said, her amicability continuing to relax me. 'Now let's see. You're looking for Hadar. It's *Yom Reshon* today, so she's in the *mifal*, I think. They'll have her *mispar* in the *chedar ochel*. I'll bring you over, if you like.'

'Thanks,' I said, pretending I had the slightest idea what she had just said. She got off her bicycle.

'I'm Sara.'

'Joseph,' I replied. 'Thanks for showing me.'

'No problem. I'm going to the *matpera* anyway.'

'Your English is very good,' I told her. 'Are you Israeli?'

'Yes, I am,' she laughed. 'But I'm originally from South Africa.'

An elderly man in a large electric wheelchair whizzed by.

'*Shalom*,' he mumbled at us as his minuscule brown and white Chihuahua raced after him, yapping aggressively at us as he passed.

'Is this a retirement village?' She stopped pushing her bicycle and looked at me.

'Why? How old do you think I am?'

'No, no, no,' I spluttered out. 'I didn't mean you. I meant...'

'Old people live here,' she explained. 'If that's what you mean.'

'No, I didn't mean that,' I fumbled. 'I meant I heard that some famous bloke retired here, and then I just saw that other chap go by and I...'

She burst out laughing. 'Some famous bloke? That's a good one. You mean Ben-Gurion?' Her South African accent was heavy on her now. 'Wait until I tell Henrik that one.'

I laughed too, only more uneasily but with quite a bit of relief.

'Where are you from?' she asked me, continuing to walk again.

'Ireland,' I told her.

'Ah,' she said, but I was unsure whether 'ah' was a good or a bad thing.

A balding man in his forties stretched his leg over his bicycle and peddled off, but not before smirking, glancing at me and saying something to Sara in Hebrew. She laughed and replied to him also in Hebrew.

This brief and apparently innocuous incident was to become a staple part of my daily life in Israel. Whether in a group or with a single friend, it was perfectly acceptable practice to converse in Hebrew without informing the non-Hebrew speaker of anything that was discussed, even if or especially if the non-Hebrew speaker was the subject of the conversation. As unintentional and even unconscious as it may well have been, it remained nonetheless rather unsettling whenever it happened. Of course, in later years, as I became proficient in this labyrinthine language, I too became guilty of these socially acceptable yet secretive conversations.

Sara shoved the front wheel of her bicycle into an empty space on a rail that held a row of about twenty bicycles.

'There's a phone that we can use in the dining room,' she told me.

The dining room was a large two-storey, rectangular building, its second floor made up almost entirely of windows. Surrounding the building were beautifully landscaped gardens, lusciously green lawns with tall perennial and deciduous trees standing guard over them, and vibrant-coloured flowers and cacti growing side by side in the stony soil. One of the lawns was being lavished with a fine and plentiful spray of water that shot twenty feet into the air, fashioning a perfectly formed rainbow, before falling gracefully onto the grass. The giant palm trees were the biggest I'd ever seen and towered over the dark green rose bushes, themselves five feet tall.

I wanted to ask Sara if this was an oasis but was afraid to pose yet another stupid question. No matter, when I turned around to speak to her, she had disappeared. I walked towards the dining room, the full-length glass doors opening automatically for me. As I placed my bag down at the base of the stairs, I could see Sara talking into an old-fashioned telephone receiver. To one side I could see a large notice board that stretched almost the entire length of the wall covered in announcements and posters for various events. A young girl, maybe nine or ten years old, was writing her name under one of the pictures, signing up for some event that seemed to involve dancing and a large violin. She was writing her name from right to left using a pen that was attached to the board with a piece of string.

'*Tanya, vamos ahora, por favor,*' a woman's voice called out in Spanish.

'*Imma, ani ba,*' she replied in Hebrew, dropping the pen and running out of the room.

The door opened to let her out and allow two tall, blonde-haired guys in. They were dusty and red-faced and wearing similar dark blue clothes – shirts that were too tight for their broad shoulders, trousers so long that they were rolled up at the bottom. They were speaking to each other in what I guessed was Russian. At the other end of the walkway was another automatic glass door. An attractive woman in her thirties with dark curly hair and brown eyes came through the door and walked over to a wall containing over one hundred small metal doors that I assumed were post boxes. Each box featured a label with Hebrew writing and a number; using a key, she opened one of the doors and removed a sheet of paper. Reading the sheet, she walked by me. Just before climbing the stairs, she glanced up and made eye contact with me.

'*Shalom.*'

'*Shalom,*' I blurted back and turned to watch her walk up the stairs.

'Ahem,' Sara coughed at me. I turned around, red-faced.

'Hadar can't leave the *mifal*... She says sorry, but she asked me to explain to you where to go, and she'll call you later.'

'How will she call me? How will she know where I am?'

'Because she told me what room you have to go to, and so I'll tell you, and then you'll know, and then she'll call you at that room.'

'Right,' I said, my face getting redder. She explained to me where the volunteer housing was located, promising me it wasn't too far.

'Thanks for your help, Sara,' I said throwing the bag over my shoulder.

'You're very welcome. I hope you enjoy your stay here.'

I looked out through the glass doors at the lawns and in the direction that I was supposed to go. I figured I'd ask Sara my stupid question. She probably thought me a little daft anyway.

'Tell me, is this an oasis?'

'No,' she laughed. 'Not at all.'

'So how come there's so much greenery here?'

'Well, apparently Ben-Gurion, one of the founding fathers of Israel who lived here – the famous guy you mentioned,' she said smiling, 'he told the workers here to bring in experts and to do an analysis of the soil. After many tests, the experts told them it would be impossible to grow anything on this land.'

'So what did they do?' I asked.

'He told the workers to fire the experts and to hire new ones.'

I walked along the cobblelock path encircling the lawns, past the vibrant rose bushes and legions of cacti. A few sandy-coloured, single-storey buildings with flat roofs nestled under the branches of numerous trees. Although the air still felt hot whenever I inhaled, it had a sweet smell, scented by the diverse amount of plants and vegetation and cooled slightly in the shade of the trees. The path was scattered with dried-out pine needles that crunched under my feet and gave off a musty smell that added to the perfumed air. In the distance, I could faintly hear what sounded like a Janet Jackson song. The cobblelock turned to concrete, and the path narrowed as it wound its way among more pine trees, their branches stooping in unison, as if shying from the sun. The ground underneath was carpeted in their brown needles and wide-open, parched pine cones. The muffled sound of music grew louder and was now accompanied by rowdy voices, followed by a child screaming and then a splash. Through the shade of the trees, I could make out the tanned bodies of people of all ages lying on sunloungers or climbing in and out of a decent-sized swimming pool, the surface of which was glistening flirtatiously.

What is this place where flowers grow out of the rocks and sandy soil, I thought to myself. Who were these people who first came here to live in a desert and work and play under an incessant sun? A people, both now and historically, besieged by an unsympathetic environment and inhospitable weather conditions. A land surrounded on all sides by hostile nations who have vowed to annihilate these people, and who, for over fifty years, have tried time after time to bring their plan to fruition. And yet here they were in temperatures of over thirty degrees in the shade listening to Janet Jackson and watching their kids jumping in and out of a swimming pool.

With the swimming pool to my left, still partially obscured by the trees, I came to a wider road, as Sara had described. A young man about my own age drove by on a well-worn tractor, the dark fumes from its rambunctious diesel engine bellowing out of its tall chimney-like exhaust; his long dark hair, not unlike the fumes themselves, blowing wildly behind him in the windowless cabin, where he bounced rhythmically up and down in his seat.

Once he had passed, and the trail of smoke and noise had cleared, I could make out three rows of, what can only be described as chalets, reminiscent of the holiday homes in Butlins where I had stayed with my family when I was a child. Each row of chalets contained four separate rooms; in front of each one was a small patio garden. Compared with the orderliness of the rest of the kibbutz, this area could probably best be described as unkempt or even squalid. A litter of bicycle parts lay strewn about on the ground. To the side was a black crater-like opening containing a half-burnt and still smouldering wooden pallet. Around this hole were makeshift chairs of plastic beer crates, a mattress from a single bed with a spring sticking out of the side, and a legless, dark grey-coloured sofa. Some empty Goldstar beer bottles were stacked neatly by the first door. A towel, some clothes and red swimwear were hanging from a plastic cord attached at one end by a nail in a doorpost and attached at the other end to the branch of an olive tree. The cord drooped down so low that half the towel was lying on the ground, covered in dust. This I reckoned had to the volunteers' accommodation – sandwiched between the outer road of the kibbutz and the perimeter fence.

Beyond that fence, or what I would soon be calling 'my back garden,' all vegetation ceased to exist, and the earth returned to its natural state. In the distant horizon, I could see a mountain range that stretched endlessly. One mountain in particular had a lighter-coloured path snaking up one side like a limpid vein that was visible even from a great distance. Running along the remaining length of the road were about twenty long, white caravans, all neatly arranged and looking as if they'd only been put there the day before: I crossed the road to the volunteers' chalets searching for room number five. Outside the door of room number one, a girl in blue shorts and a purple T-shirt was sitting on a kitchen chair in the shade reading a thick paperback. She didn't notice me, and not wanting to disturb her, I figured that number five must be in the next row of chalets. This was good as that particular row faced the fence and an expanse of desert. Number five had a little garden outside the door. There had been an attempt, either unsuccessful or simply abandoned, to grow vegetables of some sort, but the green leaves of whatever plant it was drooped down limply, as if disappointed with the effort of it all. I knocked and opened the door.

'Hello.'

I got no answer. Two guys in their early twenties, sitting up in their respective beds, looked up to see who was disturbing them. The accommodation consisted of just one room, with a bed pushed up against each of the three walls, one of which was being used as a table-cum-storage area. I guessed that this was supposed to be my bed. The room was dark; three low-wattage lamps hung on the wall over each bed. At the end of one of the beds stood a monster-sized fridge so completely covered in graffiti that its original colour was impossible to decipher.

'Ye all right?' one of the lads asked in a heavy Scottish accent. He had a well-read Stephen King novel in one hand and was propped up on his elbow. His hair was fair and curly but retreating from his forehead as if subtlety dissociating itself from the face below. He had vivid blue eyes that seemed all the more intense, surrounded as they were by a bright red, sunburnt face.

'How's it going?' I said. 'I was told to come to this room. Hadar I think it was.'

'Oh, right,' the Scottish guy said looking over at the other bed. 'Let me get this shit off the bed for you.'

He stood up and offered me his hand. 'I'm Aengus, by the way.'

'Joseph,' I told him. 'Sorry you've got to move your stuff.'

'Nay bother, lad,' he said starting to move all the clothes and bags from my bed onto his own.

'How's it going, mate?' said the other guy in a cockney accent and stuck out his hand. 'Charlie.'

'Hey, Charlie,' I said. 'Sorry if I'm cramping your space a bit.'

'Don't worry about it mate. And by the way, you've only been in the room thirty seconds and you've already apologised twice.'

'Did I?' I said smiling. 'Sorry.'

He responded with a big toothy grin. He was a little older than Aengus and had a confidence about him that bordered on smart arse. This I hoped wouldn't cause us any friction, seeing as how I was at times a smart arse myself. He was wearing a pair of dark blue, canvas trousers, which by now I was beginning to suspect were some kind of kibbutz work uniform. His shirtless torso revealed a deep tan and a tattoo of a lion holding a sword in one paw and a shield with the red cross of St George in the other. He was also sporting a bit of a beer belly, which was evident even when he was lying down. His hair was short, brown and plain, his eyes blue and intelligent.

'An Englishman named Charlie and a Scotsman named Aengus. I kind of feel bad my name's not Patrick or Paddy.'

'Sounds like the opening line of a joke,' Aengus said. 'An Englishman, a Scotsman and an Irishman were in the desert...'

'We could call you Paddy,' Charlie suggested.

'Perhaps not,' I said looking at him.

'Fair enough mate,' he replied.

I threw my elongated bag onto the bed, happy not to have to pick it up again for at least a few months.

'Fancy a beer?' Charlie asked.

'Deadly, yeah,' I said.

'I don't know what deadly means, but there's some beer in the fridge if you fancy one.'

'Thanks.'

The fridge at the end of his bed took up a large proportion of the room. It was a retro-style affair, as if plucked from an appliance-filled kitchen of a 1950s American horror movie. Among the wide selection of graffiti were offerings such as 'Johnny, Melbourne, 1986', 'Henri – Marseille', 'I hate the fucking chicken house', and 'Jimmy – July 1990'. When I opened the heavy door, which seemed to comprise half the fridge, all I could see were about six or eight beers inside a small igloo-type opening: a wall of solid, white ice filled almost all of the rest of the available space. There were two types of beer: Tuborg and Goldstar.

'What's this Goldstar stuff?' I asked.

'It's the local brew,' Charlie said.

'Any good?' I asked.

'Ey, it's fuckin' great stuff,' Aengus said, and Charlie nodded in agreement.

I opened the beer and sat on my bed to drink it. It was ice-cold and tasted amazing. The bed was a single, military-style creation, but after sleeping in a different bed every night for the previous two weeks, I was happy to call this one my own. The room was square, about twelve feet by twelve feet with two windows – one above my bed and the other above the sink in the small kitchenette at the entrance. At the end of Charlie's bed were five built-in wardrobes, the doors of which were decorated with various graffiti designs. The bathroom was functional – toilet, sink and a decent-sized shower.

'Have you been travelling a bit?' Charlie asked me.

'Yeah, just for a few months though,' I told him. 'Why? Do I have a travel-weary look about me?'

'No, it's just there aren't too many people coming straight from the British Isles with a tan.'

I ignored this geographical and political faux pas for the sake of maintaining a harmonious household.

'Our Charlie's a bit of a Sherlock Holmes,' Aengus said.

'Are you Watson then, Aengus?' Charlie asked.

'Probably more Doyle than Watson,' I said.

'What?' Charlie asked.

'Well, Watson was English but the author Arthur Conan Doyle was Scottish. Edinburgh, I think,' I said.

'I think he has you there,' Aengus said.

'Fair enough,' he conceded. 'But he spent most of his life in London.'

'So did Oscar Wilde,' I said. 'But he was still Irish.'

'Oscar Wilde was Irish?' Aengus asked. 'I didn't know that.'

'Did you know he was gay?' Charlie asked him.

'Ey,' he said. 'I've heard that rumour all right.'

'Did you?' Charlie asked him, sitting up on his bed. 'Who'd you hear that from?'

'Don't know. I just read it somewhere.'

'Well, it's just gossip,' Charlie said. 'I wouldn't go spreading it about.'

'I wasn't going to,' Aengus assured him. 'The man's entitled to his privacy.'

'That's decent of you,' Charlie told him.

'What the man gets up to in his own home is of nay business of mine,' Aengus said. 'Whether he's a sausage jockey or nay a sausage jockey.'

'Jesus Christ,' Charlie said turning to me. 'You see what I've had to put with for the last four weeks.'

The phone rang.

'The Oscar Wilde Appreciation Club,' Charlie said answering it. 'No, only joking, Hadar... Yes, he's here beside me... See you later.'

He handed the phone to me.

'Hello,' I said.

'Hi Joseph. This is Hadar,' said a female voice whose accent I couldn't place. 'I'm sorry I couldn't come down to meet you when you arrived.'

'That's fine, Hadar.'

'Anyway, I'm sure the two boys there are full of information.'

'They're a great help, all right,' I said to her, looking at Charlie who was reaching for another beer while Aengus was picking the dirt out of his toenails.

'Good, good,' she said. 'You're going to be sharing with them. There's a group arriving soon, and I want to try and keep as many rooms as possible empty.'

'That's fine,' I told her looking at Aengus, who was now closely examining the newly plucked contents of his toenails.

'Now, it's laundry this evening so you can go to Helga and get some supplies from her. Charlie will tell you where to go.'

'For fuck's sake,' Charlie shouted at Aengus. 'That's fucking disgusting.'

'Okay, thanks,' I said.

'You can get the fuck out of my room if you're going to do that,' Charlie continued.

'Is everything okay there?' Hadar asked.

'It's nay your room,' Aengus shouted back at him. 'It's our room.'

'Everything's fine, Hadar,' I told her.

'Well, it's a filthy fucking habit,' Charlie said.

'Okay, she opens between six and seven. Just tell her I sent you.'

'I never say anything about your smelly feet, do I?' Aengus asked.

'That's great,' I told her. 'I'll be there.'

'My feet?' Charlie continued. 'We've the only room in the place with no cockroaches 'cause of your stinking fucking boots at the front door.'

'Also, you'll be marked up for work tomorrow,' Hadar continued. 'But one of the lads there will show you where to look up your name on the board.'

'Well, at least they're outside the room, unlike your fuckin' feet,' Aengus said.

'Thanks, Hadar,' I said.

'I'm sure I'll get to meet you in the next day or two, Joseph.'

'Keep it up, Scottie,' Charlie warned. 'You'll be joining your stinking boots outside soon enough.'

'That's great, thanks,' I said, and hung up the phone.

'Nay bother with me, pal,' Aengus said standing up grabbing the bottle of beer out of Charlie's hand. 'And I'll take my beer with me.'

With that, Charlie launched himself at Aengus, the two of them wrestling each other to the floor as I sat on the side of my bed wondering what on earth kind of a place I'd come to.

4

After talk of Charlie moving to another room and Aengus staying, and then Aengus moving out and Charlie staying, followed by a discussion about some sort of Hadrian's Wall being built in the centre of the room using adhesive tape and two wooden pallets, Charlie eventually got bored, called Aengus a 'wanker', and fell asleep. Aengus continued to complain about Charlie – more vigorously now that Charlie was asleep. But he was careful enough to glance in his direction every now and again before adding 'and every other English cunt I've ever met'. He went on to lament about what he wouldn't give for something called a 'fish supper', finally adding that if 'that Argentinian bitch' put him working in the orchards one more time he was either going to get third-degree burns or be 'completely fucking vaporised' by the 'poxy sun'. I wanted to ask Aengus a lot of questions about the kibbutz, but I thought it better to wait until he had cooled down a bit. Mind you, his face was so sunburnt that it was impossible to say whether his face was inflamed with rage and animosity, or simply just inflamed.

'Tell me, Aengus,' I eventually asked him. 'How come there are so many different nationalities here? How are they all Israeli?'

'Any Jew in the world can come here and claim citizenship. It's called the right to return or something. I'm not sure.'

'Are you Jewish?'

'You taking the piss, son?' he asked me. 'My mother's Catholic and my dad's Church of Scotland. To be honest with you, I've no fucking idea what that makes me, but I know it doesn't equal being Jewish. Why? Are you?'

'Jewish? No.'

'Well, you look more Jewish than me anyways. I'm an accountant from Edinburgh, and that's exactly what I look like.'

I suppose if someone were to force me to draw a picture of an accountant from Edinburgh I would draw a likeness not dissimilar in appearance to Aengus.

'So why are you here?' I asked him.

'Why are you here?' he replied.

'I thought I knew, but I'm not sure now.'

'Then, I'm not too sure either,' he said smiling.

'Fair enough.'

'Listen, mate, I started work at five this morning in the orchards and if that wagon has put me back there again, that means I need to get some serious shut eye pronto, and I suggest you do the same, so if you don't mind.' He threw his Stephen King book on the floor and lay back on his bed.

'Just one more thing,' I said.

He didn't open his eyes. 'Go for it.'

'What's the work sheet that Hadar said I'd be written down on?'

'When we go to eat this evening in the dining room I'll show you,' he promised, yawning profusely. 'It'll tell you where you'll be working tomorrow and at what time. Most of the jobs are all right. Except maybe the chicken house. Or the poxy orchards for two weeks in a row.'

He mumbled something about Argentina, the Falklands and various large farm animals and nodded off to sleep.

The dusty shutters on the outside of the window above my head were closed, but I could still feel the intensity of the heat permeating the room. Gaps in the shutters revealed glimpses of an ardent white light, as if it were trying to squeeze its way into the room. I put my bag on the floor at the foot of the bed, just then realising that the bed consisted of a thin mattress on a metal frame; there were no sheets, blankets or even a pillow. A small white fan on the floor beside Charlie's bed swirled almost noiselessly, rotating from side to side gracefully, as if obediently standing guard over Charlie while he slept. I took off my shoes, pulled out an old T-shirt from the top of my bag, rolled it into a ball to create a pillow, and lay down on my back. Whether it was the hypnotic sound of the gentle swishing back and forth motion of the fan, or whether it was because I was genuinely exhausted, I fell almost instantly into a deep sleep.

When I awoke, I found Charlie staring down at me. I had no idea either who he was or where I was.

'It's half six, mate. You'll be late if you don't go now. Best not to piss off Helga on your first day.'

Since my current whereabouts were such a mystery to me, any pressing future appointments were beyond my comprehension. I had been dreaming of ships sailing through the desert, the sands parting like waves, when Charlie's voice broke through my sleep: I thought he was a pirate and raised my hands in protest.

'You've got to get a move on, mate,' he said, shaking my shoulder. I opened my eyes fully and turned to look around the room. Aengus was still asleep, his mouth wide open, snoring erratically. Charlie walked over to his bed and winking at me, stood over him, looking down.

'Hey, Scottie, Scottie, Scottie,' he said, badly mimicking a Scottish accent. While trying to stifle his laughter, he unzipped his trousers and stood in his underwear, leaning directly over Aengus's snoring head.

'Would ye fancy a wee drop of Iron Bru?' he said, grabbing his crotch and lowering himself closer to Aengus's face, which continued snoring empathically.

'A nice wee drop, eh laddie?' he said, louder this time.

Aengus suddenly stopped snoring, blinked and then opened his eyes fully.

'Will ye have a wee bit of cock for your tea, me laddie?' Charlie said, laughing loudly now. Aengus let out a loud shriek, a cry not unlike what you'd expect to hear emanating from a twelve-year-old schoolgirl, and jumped up. Charlie fell back onto his own bed in a fit of laughter, but Aengus wasn't impressed in the least.

'There's something wrong with you, boy,' he screamed at Charlie, his Scottish accent even stronger than earlier.

'That's nay right,' he continued. 'Ye dinnae go sticking your nob in another man's face while he's trying to get a wee bit of fuckin' shut eye.' But the more Aengus screamed, the louder Charlie laughed, almost asphyxiating himself in convulsions.

I looked at my watch. It was twenty minutes to seven.

'Shit,' I said. 'I have to go.'

'You're nothing but a Cockney shirt lifter. Do ye hear me?' Aengus told him.

'Where do I go for my bed sheets and stuff?' I asked them.

Charlie tried to regain some sort of composure. 'Sorry, mate,' he said. 'Go back towards the swimming pool; do you know where that is?'

'Yes,' I said.

'At the gate of the pool, there's a bomb shelter painted blue.'

'There's a what?' I asked.

'A bomb shelter,' he said. 'They're all over the place here. You'll know it when you see it. It's blue and that's the entrance. Just go in there and down the steps.'

'Okay, thanks,' I said and ran out the door, not knowing exactly where I was going.

'You need professional psychiatric help, Charlie,' Aengus was telling him as I left. 'I'm nay joking you.'

'Oh, lighten up, Scottie. What's one wee cock in the face between friends, eh?'

'And stop calling me Scottie,' I could hear Aengus yelling from outside the room. 'My name's Aengus.'

It was still warm outside but noticeably cooler than it had been earlier on. The sun wasn't visible, and the sky was still a bright blue but turning darker on the eastern horizon. Two guys in shorts were crouched down over the scorched and discoloured patch of ground, trying to rekindle the smouldering and blackened wood, while a third guy stood watching them, holding a bottle of Goldstar. They didn't notice me, but a girl outside one of the rooms, shaking the sand out of a pair of boots, looked up as I passed and smiled. She had short, mousy brown hair and was wearing a purple T-shirt inside out. I waved as I passed and she nodded back at me. I crossed the road and made my way towards the gates of the pool.

A blue, triangular-shaped, concrete construction jutted out of the ground like the tip of an iceberg. While not completely hidden from view, it stood in the centre of about twenty trees, their high branches ensuring that the bomb shelter entrance was kept in constant shade. The bulky door at the entrance was painted a dull, matte grey; lever-like handles were welded on the front and back. My footsteps echoed as I descended the concrete stairs.

'Hello,' I called out.

'Hallo,' a woman's voice called back.

At the bottom of the stairs was a single room with a grey painted concrete wall; the entire area was illuminated by a single white fluorescent bulb. It was an Aladdin's cave of bed sheets and blankets; clothes, mostly either cobalt blue or army green; coats and jackets; heavy winter sweaters; black boots and various coloured trainers; and a wall of pillows stacked from floor to ceiling. It took me almost a full minute of looking around to realise that standing in the middle of the room was a woman smiling up at me.

'Hallo,' she said again. Her thick German accent was already obvious by virtue of her use of this one prosaic word.

'Hi,' I replied and made my way down the remaining few steps.

She was about five feet tall, in her early sixties, and had slivers of darkness in her otherwise white, curly hair.

'Can I help you?' she asked.

'I just got here today. Hadar sent me,' I said apologetically.

'Goot, goot, ya. My name is Helga Hirsch,' she said. I couldn't imagine her having any other name.

'You vill need everything, I presume?'

'If everything includes bed sheets and a pillow, then yes please.'

'Okay, goot. Now let me see,' she said and took out a heavy black folder that had a large, red 'V' ominously marked on the cover. She placed it on the table in front of her and ran a finger through the English, German and Hebrew handwritten text, as if seeking out some devious and esoteric spelling. She punched a spot on a page with her index finger and lifted her head to look at me, then looked back at her finger.

'Vhy not?' she said, to herself more than to me, and took up her pencil. 'Name?'

I was unsure whether she was even talking to me.

'Vat is your name?' she said, this time turning her head towards me.

'Oh, sorry. Joseph. My name's Joseph.'

'Vell, Joseph. You are now volunteer number thirteen. So, from now on, vit your vork schedule and your *cartis verod* and of course on all of your clothes and bed sheets, vill be written "V13". You understand?'

'Unlucky for some,' I said jokingly.

'Vat?'

'Thirteen, it's an unlucky number. I was just making a joke.'

'Ah,' she said. 'A joke. I see, but you are wrong. In ancient Judaism culture, it is a very lucky number. Your time on this kibbutz will be blessed.'

'Great,' was my succinct answer.

She turned and made eye contact with me. Suddenly, I could hear the slight buzzing from the overhead light, could feel the stillness in this tiny room buried twenty feet underground, and noticed we were both breathing in unison.

'It is a magical number, Joseph. Very magical,' and then she clapped her hands, closed the book and marched over to a pile of blue shirts, folded neatly on a shelf.

For pedantic and punctilious readers like myself who take acute pleasure from such banality as lists and details, this is what I left the room with:

Two pairs of navy shorts
One pair of trousers
Two short-sleeved shirts
One long-sleeved shirt
One pair of ankle-high boots
An assortment of five T-shirts

A long black coat with a high collar and lined with white fur of dubious origins. I queried the necessity for a coat but she assured me that the mornings would start to get colder, and that I would thank her for it later.

A blue canvas hat for the sun

A small-net bag made of material similar to that used in string vests, with a tie that had the ingenious, if somewhat unenviable, job of retaining my underwear and socks, while they happily bounced around inside an industrial-sized washing machine

Two bed sheets

One blanket

One pillow and case

Before I left the room, everything was branded with sticky tabs using a hot iron and a permanent marker to create a capital letter 'V' and its ambiguous partner '13'. I said my thanks and left, but as I climbed the stairs unsteadily laden down with my loot, she called out to me, 'Good luck, Vee thirteen.' I turned around, but she already had her back to me, her head buried in her folder, scribbling in at least one of her three languages.

When I stepped outside, I was surprised to find it was already dark. In Israel, the dusk is more of a fleeting visitor than a lingering guest. I felt a little as if the day had been prematurely stolen from me, like the remaining bites of an unfinished meal. I even felt a little disorientated in the darkness as I struggled with a tower of textiles which partially obscured my vision and caused me to drop various items along the way, forcing me to squat down precariously to retrieve them.

Back in my room, I managed to safely open and close the door with my leg before tripping over Aengus's Stephen King novel in the middle of the floor. Luckily, I fell onto my bed, while the mountain of clothes and sheets exploded into the air.

'You all right, mate?' Aengus asked me from his bed.

'I'm okay, thanks,' I said and started picking up the fabric shrapnel around the room.

The door of the bathroom opened, as steam and the smell of deodorant bellowed out into the room. In the midst of this fog, Charlie appeared, dressed and fresh looking, clapping his hands. 'So, are we going for something to eat?'

The three of us made our way back to the dining room. The air was filled with contagious stillness, an almost meditative calm, as if the plants and the ground itself were sighing in relief at having survived another tortuous day under the reign of a lordly sun. Charlie offered me a cigarette as we walked. I pulled one out from a soft, paper-like, green packet, the same cigarettes as I had seen being smoked by the soldiers. It felt a little rougher on my throat than what I was used to.

'What brand is this?'

'It's the local shite. The kibbutz gives you five packs a week for free. The other brand is better though. It's called Time. They say the crap that falls off the conveyer belt when they're making Time cigarettes is swept up and used to make this shit.'

'So why smoke these?'

'Cause the name of the cigarettes suits our Charlie,' Aengus cut in.

I looked at the name – Noblesse.

'Nob less,' Aengus said laughing.

'It's pronounced Nooobless, you fucking twat,' Charlie told him. 'The other brand's in a white box with poncey white filters on them and unless you want everyone to think you're a poofter, like they do Aengus here, then it's best sticking to a man's cigarette.'

'Nobody thinks I'm a bender,' Aengus shouted.

'Oh, yeah?' Charlie said. 'So how come you haven't even shagged one bird yet, and you've been here for four weeks already?'

'I'm biding my time, smart arse,' he replied. 'I don't just jump into the sack with every drunken slapper in the place. Unlike you, I have a few different requirements when it comes to who I get into bed with.'

'Really?' Charlie asked. 'And what requirements are they then? That they have a cock and balls?'

Aengus's face went red.

'You haven't even got a shag off Jenny,' Charlie persisted. 'And everyone's had a go on her. Even Lizzie the lesbian.'

'Maybe that's why? 'Cause I don't fancy a dose of something and I'm not a lesbian,' Aengus said. 'I'll give you my free ciggies from now on, if you like, Joe. So fuck you, Charlie boy.'

'Cheers,' I said.

'It's a dirty and unhealthy habit anyway,' he added.

'And taking one up the arse is hardly the healthiest of pastimes either, Aengus, but that doesn't seem to stop you.'

'I'm nay gay, you prick,' Aengus screamed at him, so loud that some people on the other side of the lawn looked over in our direction.

'Any other perks or freebies?' I asked in an attempt to ease the hostilities.

'Yeah, free condoms,' Charlie replied. 'But you can have Aengus's supply of them as well.'

The dining room was on the floor above the reception area where I had been earlier. The top of the stairs opened up on to a large corridor, which in turn led to a large dining area with five rows of tables and chairs; each row had four tables and each table eight chairs. In the corridor were two long stainless steel steam tables displaying metal trays containing hot food such as rice and vegetables. At the other end were tin basins of uncut salad, individually arranged: tomatoes, onions, peppers, lettuce and cucumbers. Behind them was some bread and a bread cutter, and to our right as we walked in, cutlery and trays. At the very end was a large water boiler for tea and coffee. The whole buffet-style arrangement had a meticulous efficiency to it; one that I imagined had remained unchanged for years.

Following Aengus and Charlie's lead, I took a tray and shuffled along behind them in the growing queue. I was undecided whether I was hungry or not, so took some rice, vegetables and tea. I later found out that there was a precedent, almost a rule, as to where you could sit. The kibbutz members sat to the right, individuals and families; younger people, soldiers, and some rebel members sat in the middle section; the volunteers sat on the farthest row on the left. I was never told this, but like many things in a kibbutz, there is an assumption that you are automatically aware of these idiosyncrasies. If, like me, you're a newbie, then you simply copy the person in front of you.

At the table, I was introduced to some of the other volunteers. They all had welcoming faces glowing with deep tans.

Hannah, the girl I had seen earlier dusting off her boots, was German. When I asked, she told me that she always wore her T-shirts inside out for 'existential and rebellious reasons' (I didn't press her on what exactly these were). She was prettier than I had remembered her.

Chad was an affable, if somewhat of a cliché Californian. He had blonde, curly hair, toned arms that showed off his tan and a ferocious appetite for rice, which he spooned into his mouth at a reckless speed. 'Dude,' is all he said with his mouth full and nodded in my direction before getting up, with empty plate in hand, and pacing back to the buffet cart.

Jenny was an almost pretty Liverpudlian in her twenties. She liked to wear tight tops that emphasised her ample breasts and, just to be sure of your attention, she also wore a necklace with a St Christopher medal which bobbed about hypnotically on her cleavage; the baby Jesus on St Christopher's shoulder perilously hanging on while gazing down at the crevice below and wearing an expression of trepidation on his ordinarily angelic face.

Markus was German with jet black eyes and tight, crinkly hair. Although his skin was quite dark, he had Caucasian features and was probably the handsomest man I had ever seen. Unfortunately for him, all aesthetic qualities vanished as soon as he opened his mouth and a cascade of complaints and whining rained down in an acerbic German accent, extinguishing any erotic flames that a starry-eyed potential female mate might have. He was the only person I've ever met, and I've met some cantankerous and acrimonious fuckers in my time, that could say 'it's a beautiful day,' and make it sound like an accusation.

Ayal was an Israeli soldier who had been temporarily suspended from the army. He was now living and working with the volunteers until such time as somebody could decide what to do with him. Two months previously, while on patrol, he had been hit in the face with a large rock and had managed to capture the stone-throwing Palestinian who had flung it at him. Rather than arrest the culprit or follow some sort of procedure, he took the attack quite personally, and stealing a Massey Ferguson digger, attempted to bury him alive on a beach in Gaza. Fortunately, a CNN reporter's curiosity got the better of her, and with her camera crew in tow, went over to investigate why and who was digging on the beach at two o'clock in the morning. Perhaps it wouldn't have been so bad if Ayal hadn't given the reporter an interview explaining exactly what he was doing, or at the very least, had not been laughing so much while doing so.

Shir was an attractive American Jewess from New York (I was unaware, at the time, of the pejorative phrase Jewish American Princess or JAP). She was very much politicised and had an unquenchable desire to let anyone who would listen know exactly how much the Jews of the world had suffered, are suffering and will happily continue to suffer for millennia to come. The rest of her time was spent tiresomely fending off the persistent sexual advances of Ayal, but with a weakening resistance and an assured knowledge of its eventual inevitability while attempting to postpone the event for as long as she possibly could.

They were an affable and welcoming bunch of individuals who had travelled much of the world, didn't sweat the small stuff, and had little or no egos to defend. The other volunteers, I was told, hadn't for various reasons come to the dining room that evening. A South African girl named Jess; a Japanese guy named Naoki; three Swedish girls named Therese, Mari-Louise and Eva; a Bostonian called Guy, and another Englishman named Robin. For most of the meal the talk was of an impending war in the Middle East, Shir laying out all possible future military scenarios. This talk was overshadowed, much to Jenny's annoyance, by the even more excited talk of a large group of Swedish volunteer girls due to arrive very soon. Aengus announced he was going downstairs to check the board to see where he was working tomorrow, and I said I'd join him.

'Are you coming over for a beer later at the fire?' Jenny asked me as I got up to leave.

'Jesus Christ, Jenny,' Charlie said. 'Give the lad a chance to unpack first.' Most at the table sniggered, except Chad who stood up with his plate and went to get more rice.

Near the dining room exit, in a sort of anteroom, was an industrial-sized dishwasher made of shiny stainless steel that shook and spewed steam and boiling water from its orifices, like some angry chained mechanical beast. Creeping along beside it was a conveyer belt of orange trays on which you put your used dishes, before they disappeared into the dishwasher's steaming mouth and were eventually spat out glistening at the other end. At the end where the clean dishes emerged stood a guy picking up the steaming hot dishes and cutlery, and then throwing them into their assigned containers. From the way he held them for a split second I could tell that each item must have been boiling hot, but he happily serenaded himself loudly with an Israeli pop song playing on a radio behind him.

'Now, that's the job you dinnae want to get, pal,' Aengus said.

'It doesn't look so bad,' I said.

'Aye, but try doing if for a whole fucking day when it's over thirty degrees outside. A fucking nightmare, I'm nay joking you.'

'*Shalom chevreh,*' (Hello friends) the dishwasher unloader yelled at us cheerfully.

We both waved at him meekly, and he went back to his singing.

'Fucking nut job,' Aengus said, under his breath, as I followed him downstairs.

'Bitch,' Aengus spat.

We were standing in front of the long notice board and reading the work sheet, which was pinned to a section of the board marked 'Volunteers'.

'I dinnae fucking believe it,' he cried. 'I swear to Christ I'm going to fucking fry out there. I'm an accountant, not a farmer. I'm not designed to pick pistachio trees. I'd never even seen a fucking pistachio in my life before I got here.'

I searched for my name and saw it written in pencil – Joseph – Chicken House Zin – 400.

'It says I'm in the chicken house,' I said. 'What's that?'

'It's shite, but if you dinnae want to work there, then just tell them that you're a vegetarian,' he advised me. 'Either way, they'll bounce you around for a week or two, to see what type of work suits you. Or what suits them, more like.'

'And what's the 400?'

'You start at four a.m.'

'Four a.m. in the morning?' I asked incredulously.

'Aye,' Aengus said. 'It's an early start all right.'

'Early?' I said. 'It's almost late, it's so early.'

'Aye, I know. I'm up at five a.m. myself.'

'And what does Charlie do?' I asked. 'I don't see his name here.'

'That prick?' he said. 'He's got one of the cushiest jobs in the place – Golda's boy. He works for Golda who's in charge of the kitchens. Plenty of nosh, indoors all day, has breaks whenever he wants to, and not only that, the place is full of Israeli chicks. Begging for it most of them are. That lazy fucker dinnae even get out of bed till seven, the prick.'

Aengus and I walked slowly back to the room. There was a bonfire raging, with some figures sitting around it drinking beers and smoking. One girl was even reading from the light of the fire.

'I'm going to say hello to the lads,' Aengus said and walked off towards the fire.

'All right,' I said. 'I'm going to go unpack and sort out my stuff.'

'See you later, so. Grab a bevvie from the fridge if you fancy one.'

When I stepped inside the room, a wave of exhaustion came over me. It was as if I had been travelling for the last two weeks just to arrive at this very room, this very bed, this very moment. I sat on the unmade bed, my clothes and belongings still packed inside my green duffle bag. The fan whined from side to side, and I could hear the crackling of the fire outside and the chattering of the voices sitting around it. I knew I should get up and take a shower; that I should unpack my bag and put everything away; that I should organise and try on my work clothes for tomorrow; that I should call home, and tell them all was well.

The last time I had called home, I had been somewhere in Italy about four or five days previously. My mother had asked me why I was still continuing with my plans when there was the possibility of a war in the region. I couldn't give her an answer without it sounding like puerile bravado, which it probably was. Whether it was the thought of a home and a family I hadn't seen for over two months and wouldn't see for several more; the realisation of being in the middle of a desert; the sense of exposure and vulnerability; the novelty and uncertainty of every single moment of my day – whatever the reason, I suddenly felt despondent and terribly alone.

I looked around the untidy room, the clothes, books and music – none of which was mine. The fan whined in my direction, and blew cool air into my face. I turned to look at it, but it turned away again as if avoiding eye contact with me.

'Yep,' I said to the fan in as cheerful a tone as I could muster. 'What the fuck am I doing here?'

5

I opened my eyes to the sound of a high-pitched cock a doodle do from somewhere in the distant darkness outside. The room was dark, and both Aengus and Charlie were asleep and snoring lightly. I had made my bed last night and promised myself that I'd unpack all my things today. Pressing the light on my watch – it read 04:30. 'Shit.' I was late.

I stumbled into the bathroom to put in my contact lenses, the light burning my tired eyes. I dressed quietly and quickly in what little light from the street lamps peeked through the shutters and groped my way blindly to the door, trying not to wake either of the lads. Just as I stepped outside, I heard Aengus's alarm clock blaring, followed by Charlie telling him to 'turn that fucking thing off' and that if he didn't he would be left with no choice but to 'shove it up your arse – sideways'.

Once outside, I ran to the road and then stopped. I was anxious not to be too late, and I was equally anxious not to make a bad first impression, but this was exactly what was going to happen as I had absolutely no idea where I was supposed to be going. The notice board had said Chicken House Zin. What or where was Zin? Even if I found a sign for Zin, I had no idea what kind of a house chickens lived in.

The cockerel crowed again.

A cockerel's a chicken, isn't it? Or is it a rooster? No, it's a hen. So is a chicken a hen?

I could see a ten-foot perimeter fence to my left and was pretty sure that the cock a doodle do had come from that vicinity. If I followed along the outside of the fence, surely I'd find an entrance and from there, the chickens. Between the fence and the road were more trees, so I had to walk very close to the fence. I could hear animal noises inside – grunts and squawks, and there was a palpable farm-like smell in the air. Up to that point in my life, my entire agricultural experience had consisted of closing the back window on my parents' car as we drove by a foul-smelling farm on a summer's evening.

I could see blurred figures moving about inside, but it was so dark away from the streetlights it was almost impossible to see anything. The cockerel crowed again, much closer this time, and I jumped with fright. Perhaps if I could just climb up and get over the fence I'd be able to talk to someone inside. I stood on some very soft ground, and my foot sank into the earth. Narrow, black, plastic water pipes were slowly dripping water for the trees; one must have snapped and partially flooded the area. I took hold of the fence and pulled my foot out of the ground. When I looked up, not twelve inches away from me was the startled face of a monkey. I yelled with fright and fell backwards onto the wet ground. I must have given the poor monkey as much of a fright as he had given me, as he began to scream his head off, jumping from branch to branch inside his cage, and waking up every sleeping beast in the place, who then joined in on the nocturnal chorus.

Still sitting on the ground, I could see the lights of a car coming in my direction. I stumbled out onto the road facing a dark-coloured jeep with spotlights mounted on the roof and on the sides, and large yellow writing in Hebrew on the doors. It stopped about ten feet from where I was standing, the headlights shining brightly on me. The driver's door opened and a man stepped out. He wore dark combat gear and had a machete strapped to his leg with black masking tape. I couldn't make out his face but in his left hand he held a torch that pointed at me, and in his right hand, not pointing at me, an Uzi submachine gun. I considered raising both my arms into the air, but thought better of it.

'*Ma ata ose po?*' (What are you doing here?)

'I'm lost. I'm looking for the chicken houses.' I can only imagine how pathetic I looked.

'Are you a volunteer?' he asked in an American accent.

'Yes, I'm supposed to be in Chicken House Zin. Is this it?'

He looked at the perimeter fence where I'd just attempted to climb.

'No,' he said. 'That's the zoo.'

As he drove me to where I was supposed to be, he told me his name was David, and he was originally from New York. He had moved to the kibbutz over twenty years earlier with his young bride Zivah, and he now only worked nights, patrolling the kibbutz from dusk till dawn. He was a good-natured man in his forties with a quick and easy laugh, and I loved his heavy New York accent that was as prominent as if he were dishing out hotdogs outside Central Park. He told me about his six children and about how proud he was that they were growing up in Israel; I wondered how he managed to produce such a large number of offspring given that he worked through the night. Later, I found out he had done a couple of tours in Vietnam when he was in the US Army, but in the true enigmatic tradition of all ex-combat soldiers in American movies, he 'didn't like to talk about it.'

As I got out of the jeep, he suggested that I confine my monkey visits to daylight hours. I laughed, shook his hand and thanked him, hoping that I would meet him again, also during daylight hours.

The kibbutz had several chicken houses constructed outside the main perimeter fence; one of these chicken houses was called Zin, and this is the one I now found myself standing outside. The compound comprised six low-level buildings, each one about one hundred metres long and twenty metres wide. All were painted white, to reflect the heat I imagined, and all had downward-facing shutters running the full length of both sides of the chicken house. At the far end of one house I could see quite a bit of activity – outdoor lights illuminating workers and a large truck in the process of being loaded with cages. Beside the truck was a door, so I headed there.

At a desk sat a man doing some paperwork.

'*Shalom*,' he said.

'Hi,' I replied. 'Sorry I'm late. I was supposed to be here at four.'

'*Tov, tov, ein baya*,' (Good, good, no problem) he said. 'Just go there, shower and change into clothes on other side.'

I had no idea why I should shower. What was wrong with the work clothes I was wearing? What other clothes did I have to put on? Sometimes, when there are simply too many questions, or when there are too many possibilities for creating misunderstandings, it's best just to wing it, so I faithfully walked towards the door where he was pointing his finger. It was indeed a changing room, with individual piles of blue clothes stacked on two benches against the walls. There were seven separate shower cubicles, one of which had the curtain pulled shut, steam rising above the person's head as they showered vigorously. On the other side of the cubicles was another changing room, this time with light brown-coloured work clothes arranged in different sizes.

I stripped and took one of the dry towels from a shelf. A therapeutic calm seeped through me as the forceful hot water ricocheted off my sleepy skin. I turned off the tap feeling alive and awake again, glad to have changed out of my muddy clothes. Towelling myself quickly, I pulled open the shower curtain and saw, standing opposite me, a blonde woman in her early twenties, changing into bra and knickers.

'Jesus,' I yelled, pulling the curtain shut again. 'I'm sorry.'

'It's okay,' she said in a Russian accent.

'I didn't know it was the ladies' shower. Sorry.'

'It's okay. You can come.'

'I beg your pardon?'

'There is no woman's and man's,' she explained. 'It is the same, you know.'

'Mixed showers?' I asked.

'Yes, yes, mixed.'

I wrapped the towel tightly around my waist and timidly pulled back the curtain again. She was still nonchalantly changing, half naked, as I busied myself looking for sizes in the various clothes that would fit me, averting my eyes as much as was physically possible. I was appalled to discover a basket of underwear that I would also have to choose an item from. As I was rummaging through the basket I came across the largest pair of Y-fronts I had ever seen.

'You must to take from the shelf,' the Russian woman said.

'What?' I asked.

'This is laundry,' she said pointing to all of the baskets that I was delving through. 'Clean is on the shelf around corner.'

I instantly dropped everything on the floor. As I was choosing another uniform, I heard the door open and then close and she was gone. I dressed quickly, cringing slightly as I put on, (clean though it was) someone else's underwear; I was surprised at my prudishness. I left by the same door as the Russian woman and walked up to where the truck was still being loaded.

Coming from a suburban background, I found the scene I encountered somewhat of a shock. The sky was still quite dark, so the working area was lit up by harsh, white spotlights. There was a lot of activity, with about fifteen people all fully engrossed in various tasks. A flatbed truck was being loaded with cages about the size of a small suitcase, each made of plastic and with holes on all sides. It wasn't until I got closer to the cages that I could see that each one was stuffed with about eight or ten live chickens. The cages themselves were tightly packed almost twenty feet high, so that they towered over the driver's cabin. The workers had to climb over the cages and on top of them in order to stack them neatly into place. Two men, working side by side, stuffed the uncooperative chickens into each cage before handing it to the next man who, in turn, passed it to the guys on the truck.

A noisy contraption that reminded me of a revolving clothes line in a dry cleaners, (except that it was fifty feet long and had over one hundred three-pronged hooks dangling from it, swinging from side to side as it rotated), was sticking out from the chicken house. Inside, a small team was responsible for choosing chickens of a particular weight and placing them unceremoniously upside down on the metal hooks, each leg in a separate holder. The weighing process involved bending down and picking up a chicken by its feet, feeling its weight in your hand and then either hooking it up or throwing it haphazardly into the air behind you, the rejected chicken squawking its displeasure and flapping its wings in protest or in an attempt to fly, before inevitably crashing to the ground.

Another team of three workers sat beside the rotating contraption wearing disposable face masks and dressed in large, plastic bibs, similar to the ones you see in a barber's shop; they were busy marking the inside back passages of the chicken with a blue dye. The reason for the plastic bibs was to provide a barrier, ineffective and all as it was, to the copious and prolific amounts of shit that the chickens were spewing out in protest against this nightmare ordeal.

What a sight! I remembered Aengus's words and went in search of the boss to instantly declare my passionate, if sudden, conversion to vegetarianism.

'Sorry, I'm late,' I told him.

'That's okay, my friend,' he said, flashing a big Argentinian smile. 'Can you help the guys on the truck?'

He turned and went back to his work, and there was nothing I could do but get to work myself. One of the guys held out his hand for me and pulled me up onto the back of the truck. Within seconds, I was being handed cages of fluttering white feathers. I was as gentle as possible with the disconcerted birds, until one stuck his claw outside a hole in the cage and sliced the top of my hand. Even still, I had empathy for the poor poultry. Just then, as I was stretching out my arms to pass a cage over my head, a shower of chicken shit cascaded down the side of my face and down my back, narrowly missing the corner of my mouth. Any remaining sympathy vanished, and I began to manhandle the cages, soon finding a rhythm to the work.

On the horizon, the sky was turning from pitch-black to light blue, proclaiming the demise of the night. Standing on the cages, I could see over the chicken houses and beyond to the barren and ancient mountains where at any moment the omnipotent sun would signal the start of a new day. The conveyer belt stopped and, suddenly, the silence of the morning became palpable, and I wondered with genuine amazement when, if ever in my entire life, I had stood and watched the sun rise.

It was about eight o'clock before all the cages were fully packed, and several thousand crammed chickens were driven out the gates. Carlos, the Argentinian boss, called for our first break, and we all piled into a small canteen where someone had already prepared a breakfast buffet for us. Now that her mask was off, I recognised Hannah, the German volunteer, as one of the 'blue dye' crew. She saw me and waved me over to where she was sitting with two others, both of whom I had already met.

There was Olga, the 'Russian girl', who actually turned out to be Ukrainian, and who, as was evident from the sniggers I could see before I sat down, had already shared her little shower room encounter anecdote with the rest of the table, and there was Shir, the American volunteer, still preaching, still political and still pretty. Breakfast was a colourful array of salads, olives and boiled eggs. The white bread was cut into thin slices and covered with a white spread that tasted more of the plastic tub than of margarine.

Hannah told me that she had already been in the kibbutz for over two months, and that she was going home in another four weeks' time. I asked her if she would miss the kibbutz and she said she would miss it very much. What, I enquired, would she miss the most? Getting up at three-thirty in the morning or looking down at a chicken's hole for eight hours a day? After Shir explained that 'hole' referred to the chicken's 'ass,' Hannah laughed hysterically, banging my shoulder with her hand and saying, '*ja, ja, der arschloch*,' before slowly sliding her hand down my arm affectionately, a gesture which was instantly noticed by both Olga and Shir, causing them to glance in each other's direction and smile, and causing me, much to my chagrin, to blush.

Shir said that she had come to the kibbutz for Zionist reasons; she was there to help Israel in any way she could and to fight Arab aggression against her homeland. Being so young and Jewish, (or maybe, I said, 'so Jewish and young'), would she not, I asked, have considered instead joining the army? Perhaps holding a gun defiantly might prove more beneficial, in the long run anyway, than holding a chicken? This, she insisted, she would love to do but, since her grandmother was coming all the way from Florida to spend Hanukkah with them in December in New York, she would have to be home by then. I told her that I doubted that Saddam Hussein would halt or even alter his Zionist bombing schedule based on her grandmother's travel arrangements, and she agreed. Either way, I'm quite sure that when the scud missiles eventually did begin to rein down on Tel Aviv in January, the good citizens of Israel fully appreciated the heart-felt concerns she expressed from the safety of the couch in her parents' twentieth-floor Manhattan apartment almost six thousand miles away.

Olga said she was from Odessa, and although she missed her family very much, she had made *aliyah*, which meant that she had come to live and work in Israel permanently. Would she have to join the army? I asked. She said that she was due to start her two-year stint in three months' time. I raised my eyebrows in Shir's direction, but unfortunately she didn't notice as she was picking up a piece of egg with her plastic fork, muttering something about what she wouldn't give right now for some pheasant coq au vin at the Waldorf Astoria on Park Avenue. Olga went on about her life story in Odessa, but every time I closed my eyes or blinked, visions of her half-naked body flickered before my closed eyes like an acid flashback and prevented me from fully concentrating on her narrative.

I'm not sure how long had passed before I realised that Hannah was tapping my arm repeatedly. I turned, bleary-eyed, to face her. She asked me if my eyes were okay as I was blinking a lot. I coughed, blamed the dust and said that I was going outside for a cigarette. She wanted to know if I was going to the volunteers' clubhouse that night; the question attracted further glances from both Olga and Shir, except this time their glances were also noticed by Hannah, and she blushed accordingly.

Now that the truck had departed, most of the workers headed for the showers. I was informed that the chickens were being transported up north somewhere, that they would be used to breed offspring which would eventually end up on dinner plates. Left behind in the now empty chicken house were the three girls, Shir, Olga, and Hannah; Ayal, obviously, as Shir was there; Naoki, the Japanese volunteer; another Israeli soldier called Eli, and myself. Carlos gave us the unenviable and dusty task of cleaning the floor, removing the dried chicken shit using wide spades and metal brushes.

Naoki worked assiduously, like a pre-programmed robot, pushing the shovel from one end of the house to the other, a task which took him about twenty minutes. Ayal had found a cushion from God only knows where, curled up into a foetal position and was fast asleep. The three girls worked in a random order, sometimes brushing the dirt to where another girl had just cleared but never in any particular direction, just wherever they happened to be standing, each one stopping when it was her turn to talk. I worked alongside Eli for most of the rest of the morning. I was happy to talk about all things new and Israeli, and he was happy to exercise his modest proficiency in the English language.

'What your name?'

'Joseph.'

'You from France?'

'No, Ireland.'

'Holland?'

'Ireland.'

'I've been to Amsterdam.'

'Great.'

'You from near there?'

'Not really.'

'I had very good time in Amsterdam.'

'I can only imagine.'

'I was high for three days.'

'How long were you there for?'

'Three days.'

'You visited... I mean, did you visit the Anne Frank museum?'

'Yes, yes, of course. And very many prostitutes.'

'Naturally.'

'Very expensive.'

'Really? How much?'

'Ten dollar.'

'That sounds cheap enough to me.'

'Not worth ten dollar.'

'What did you, em... what did you get for that much?'

'Tour of house, and eh, where she hide.'

'Eh?'

'Where Nazis find her.'

'Oh, I see. I thought you meant...'

'What?'

'I thought the hookers were expensive.'

'No, no, prostitutes cheap and very good. I fuck every day.'

'That's lovely.'

'Sometimes four times a day.'

'Well, it certainly sounds like you had a busy schedule.'

'You want to get high or you want to fuck, you go to Amsterdam.'

'I think she actually wrote that in her diary.'

'I can't believe you never been and you from Holland.'

'Ireland.'

'Yes, yes.'

This went on for quite some time until he started telling me about his time in the army, the word 'army' being always preceded with an emphatic 'God damn fucking.' The boys, he told me, were enlisted for three years and the girls for two. There was also the option to add another year and these soldiers were sent first to a kibbutz for a year, after which they spent six months in basic training, and then the remaining two and a half years going from the kibbutz to army duty. This was the option that he and the rest of the soldiers in his squad had chosen. He was in his third year and was due back in four months at a camp near Jenin, a town on the West Bank. The girls were usually given lighter duties but, lately, were assuming a more combative role alongside the boys. Girls were also quite often used as training officers, he told me, as it was harder for the boys to give up or quit during a training session if there was a girl screaming orders at them.

Carlos eventually arrived back just before noon, the end of our working day, telling us to finish up, shower and head for lunch. All of us took credit for Naoki's labours, even Ayal, who was woken up by Shir when she saw Carlos approaching.

'By the way,' I asked Eli, as we left. 'How do you say thanks in Hebrew?'

'*Tankim*,' he said.

'*Tankim*,' I repeated. 'It's good to know at least a few words.'

'Yes, yes,' he said, looking at me a little puzzled.

In the changing rooms, Shir refused to shower until all the men were finished, whereupon Eli stripped off and started to shower in front of her with the curtain open. The three girls laughed and screamed like schoolgirls and ran back out into the sun. When we had finished and were standing outside in the sun, Ayal said he wanted to wait for the girls; Eli on the other hand just shrugged and walked off. Naoki and I stood there for maybe five seconds, feeling the thirty degrees plus sun on our heads, and quickly took off after him.

For about twenty minutes, on a well-worn desert track, we walked in silence until we came to the perimeter fence of the kibbutz. Here, the road turned to concrete and the desert turned to grass. A long road stretched before us, at the end of which I knew lay the car park and the bus stop where I had arrived the previous day. Beyond that was the dining room, where we were now headed. On our right, we passed a large corrugated iron building, in front of which was a yard bursting with partially dismantled and rusting tractors as well as work vehicles of various makes, shapes and colours. Door-less trucks, engine-less machinery and tractor arms suspended in mid-air all crammed together like an exotic garden of bizarre, metallic plants and flowers.

I asked Eli if it was a garage workshop.

'*Ken, ken, ha mosach*,' he said. 'The garage.'

A blonde curly haired guy was using a steam cleaner to wash a car near the front door. Eli screamed at him in Hebrew, laughing as he did so, but the guy didn't reply, either because he was deafened by the steamer or simply because he chose to ignore Eli. Or maybe it was a bit of both. The next building was similar in size only closer to the road and without a yard, but with giant rose bushes standing guard on either side of the open door. It took too long for my eyes to adjust fully due to the intensity of the brightness outside, but I could make out the shadowy outlines of three figures sitting around a table scattered with coffee cups. The wide doors at the back of the building were also open. In stark contrast to the darkness inside, I could see a glorious vista of undulating hills and blue skies, the whole scene reminiscent of an enormous vibrant painting surrounded on all four sides by the black-framed interior.

'*Ha massgeria*,' Eli said. 'Metal shop.'

'What do they do in there all day?' I asked.

'That's what they do,' he said, nodding in the direction of the three men who were sitting around a table and chatting and drinking coffee.

The final building, before reaching the open space of the car park was the smallest of the three. '*Ha nagaria*,' Eli told me without being asked. 'Wood shop.'

Just inside the door, a middle-aged man with a beard was tapping a hammer against a chisel, carefully carving out a piece of wood.

'That's Jossi,' Eli said. 'Three weeks ago, his son was shot in Ramallah. But he's not dead. He's okay now.'

'It's a dangerous position in Israel,' I said.

'Yes, yes, being a soldier very dangerous,' Eli said.

'No,' I said. 'Being a carpenter's son.'

Opposite the wood shop was an electrical repair shop.

'*Hashmalia*,' Eli told me.

The whole kibbutz, or at least the bits of it I had seen thus far, reminded me of a board game that we used to play as children. It was a little self-sustained village, where everyone – the cook, the nurse, the mechanic – had their roles, and they all had their little place of business where they happily spent their day following an ostensibly pleasant, neighbourly, utopian way of life – the board game I mean.

At twelve-thirty the dining room was full to capacity, but the kitchen and dining room staff worked industriously to keep supplies moving. A young boy at a food counter plopped some sort of meat and pastry dish onto my plate.

'*Tankim*,' I said.

He merely looked back at me with a nonplussed stare, so I just assumed he was a somewhat unsociable person. Whatever other dishes I thought looked half-decent or familiar I scooped onto my plate. Spotting Aengus sitting at a faraway table, I shuffled my way over to him. The huge windows dominating the room delivered panoramic views of rich, green gardens and the desert landscape beyond the kibbutz.

'Are you all right there, Joe?' Aengus asked. 'Are you in the mood for a wee bit of chicken?'

'Very funny, Aengus,' I said, looking down at the concoction on my plate.

'This is Guy, by the way,' Aengus said, nodding to the dark-haired man sitting opposite him. He looked more like an American than any other American I'd ever seen.

'Hi,' he said, dispelling any possible doubt.

'Hello,' I said. 'What part of the States are you from?'

'Have you ever been to the States?' he asked.

'No.'

'So why ask which part?'

'I don't know,' I said. 'Just curious, I suppose.'

'Why is it that whenever I tell people I'm from the States, they always ask me what part?' he asked, raising his voice and addressing everyone at the table. 'If you're from France or Germany or even Ireland, I'd never ask you which part of Ireland you come from, 'cause it wouldn't make any fucking difference if you said Dublin or Belfast or wherever. You know what I'm saying?'

I wasn't sure if he was asking me specifically whether I knew what he was saying or not, or if it was directed to the table in general, so I just nodded noncommittally anyway. Eli sat in beside me and immediately started to shovel food into his mouth in a ferocious manner.

'Do you know Guy?' I asked him. Keeping his head down, he raised his eyes momentarily in Guy's direction.

'Hi,' Eli said in his deep voice.

'Hi,' Guy replied.

'Guy's from the United States,' I told Eli. All eyes fell on Eli and then on Guy. Eli put down his fork and filled his cup with water from the plastic pitcher on the table.

'Okay,' he said, shrugging, and started to shovel up his pile of food again. Everyone at the table smiled. Except Guy.

'I can't eat this shite anymore,' Aengus said, throwing his knife and fork onto the plate. 'Every day it's salads and vegetables. I need proper food.'

'Salads are good for you,' Guy offered.

'But it's not food,' Aengus replied. 'I want food. Not what food eats.'

With that Charlie came bounding over to our table.

'All right, ladies?' he asked.

'Here fuckin' Delia Smith,' Aengus spat at him. 'I want to put in a formal complaint about the standard of nosh is this institution.'

'Oh, yeah?' Charlie asked. 'And what seems to be the problem Mr Davidson?'

'It's shite,' Aengus said. 'That's the problem. I'm fucking withering away to my bones here. I don't feel well. It's not right, man.'

'You are looking a little pale all right, Aengus,' Charlie said laughing, and then turning to the table. 'Couldn't go to sleep last night 'cause the room was so bright with his big red head glowing.'

Everyone laughed except Guy and Eli, whose plate was now almost empty.

'Here, Joseph. These are for you, mate,' Charlie said and handed me five acrogrammes, which, he explained, were given to us every month so that we could write home for free. They were light blue and about the size of an A5 sheet that folded over onto itself and then could be sealed and the address placed on the outside. He also handed me a white sealed envelope with my name on the front, spelled 'Josef'.

'Looks like you've got to go for a jab,' he told me. Apparently, every volunteer was required to give a blood sample that was then tested for the AIDS virus. I am opposed to volunteering my blood, but in this case it looked as if I would be unable to avoid it. I read the piece of paper inside the envelope; an appointment had already been arranged for after lunch that day.

'Fuck this, I'm going to get something to eat in Beersheba later,' Aengus said. 'I've to go and get some film anyway.'

'Some what?' Guy asked.

'Film,' Aengus said.

'What the hell is fill-um?' Guy asked.

'Film,' said Aengus angrily. 'For my fucking camera. Film.'

'Oh, film,' Guy replied.

'And a fucking kebab, proper scran,' he said, turning back to Charlie. 'Anyway, Esther Rantzen, what has you so fucking perky?'

'No reason,' Charlie said. 'Just generally happy to be in your company.'

'Aye,' Aengus said slyly. 'I'd be a bit more cheerful myself if I spent most of my day poncing aboot with all the girlies in the kitchen. "Oh, Charlie, can you lift this for me?" "Charlie, can you chop this for me?" "Charlie, can you scratch my left tit?"'

With that, a heavy Argentinian man with a huge, black beard covering most of his face walked up to the table.

'*Yalla*, Aengus, Guy,' he said.

'Coming now, Miguel,' Aengus said. Miguel turned around and walked towards the door and Aengus stood up, lifting his tray and full plate of food off the table.

'I suppose you're going back to the room for a bevvy or a bit of kip?' he said to me.

'I suppose,' I said.

He looked at me and then from me to Charlie. 'Pricks,' he spat and walked off, with Guy carrying his own tray trailing behind him.

I left soon after Aengus, and met Shir and Olga on the stairs, with Hannah a couple of steps behind them. 'Took your time, girls?' I asked them.

'Yes,' Shir answered, rubbing up against Olga. 'We took our time showering together.' All three laughed as they passed by me.

'I only watched,' Hannah said, then leaned in and whispered to me. 'I prefer boys.' I turned and watched her climb the stairs, aware that she knew I was watching her.

As I walked outside from the air-conditioned dining room, I wondered if a day would ever come when I would get used to the heat. It was like standing in front of a bonfire, or having a soft, sizzling hot pillow smash into your body. The clinic was close by, of course – everything was close by on the kibbutz. I went into the waiting room, which was small and empty. After a few minutes, a petite woman in her forties came in.

'*Shalom*,' she said.

'Hello,' I replied, offering her the page in my hand. 'I got this note that I needed to get an AIDS test.'

'Oh, right. You're a new volunteer,' she said, in a soft Scottish accent. 'Where are you from, son?'

'Ireland.'

She took the note from my hand and looked me up and down. 'I'm a bit too busy today to be giving the Irish blood tests,' she said folding the page and putting it into her pocket. 'I'm sure you're fine.'

I walked back out into the heat, unscathed. By the time I got back to my room, the shirt on my back was hot to touch.

Beside the front door, someone had left out a yellow towel to dry; it had stiffened so much in the sun it resembled a thin sheet of cardboard. I brought it inside and stood it up against the wall.

I took one of Aengus's cold beers from the fridge, said 'sláinte' to the empty room and downed the bottle in one go. I stripped and lay on the unmade bed, my head suddenly buzzing with the beer, my strange day with chickens, the camaraderie of new friends, a few thoughts of home and many thoughts of a pretty German girl and where all of that might lead.

I closed my eyes to quieten my mind and instantly fell into a deep sleep.

6

I had forgotten to take out my contact lenses, so when I woke up a few hours later, my eyes were dry and sore. With the sand, dust and general dryness of the air, I knew that I couldn't afford to treat my eyes so carelessly from now on. I was happy though to see from the window that there was still some brightness left in the day. Charlie had his head buried inside an open bag.

'Sorry, mate,' he said, when he saw me looking at him. 'Hope I didn't wake you.'

'No, you're fine,' I said. 'I was hoping it wouldn't be dark already.'

Aengus was sleeping with his mouth open, snoring lightly. His face looked even redder than yesterday. Charlie looked over at him.

'I think Sean Connery's title of Sexiest Man in Scotland might be in jeopardy,' he said. I tried to stifle my laughter, but we both started giggling.

'Where are you off to?' I asked him.

'Cashier. Need to top up on my pink card.' He explained that the kibbutz didn't use cash in the shop or in the pub. Instead, you put credit on a card which happened to be pink, hence the name. Whenever you bought something, the person would deduct the amount and initial the card. A small allowance of a few hundred shekels was added to your pink card every month as payment for working on the kibbutz.

'I've only got twelve shekels on my card,' he said. 'And it's pub tomorrow night.'

I got up and went with him to get my own pink card. He told me the pub was only open two nights a week, Tuesdays from nine-thirty till midnight, and Fridays from ten till about two in the morning. On Fridays, there was also a disco.

'I hear you and Hannah are hitting it off,' he said, as we walked along.

'Oh yeah?' I asked. 'Where did you hear that?'

'Bumped into them in the dining room at lunchtime,' he said. 'Like the three witches in *Macbeth*, they were. Only short of a cauldron, the amount of scheming going on.'

'Gossiping were they?'

'Listen mate,' he said. 'In case you didn't notice, we don't have a telly, so, if you're looking for a bit of soap opera, gossiping is as good as it gets. There's no *Eastenders* or *Neighbours* here to chat about. Only real people. Not sure which is worse, to be honest. Gossiping about each other or giving a toss whether Dirty Den and Angie are going to get back together.'

'What are the Israeli girls like?' I asked.

'Jesus, you've got to pace yourself, mate,' he laughed. 'Work your way through the German front first.'

'No, seriously,' I said. 'Have you had any luck with them?'

'Wasting your time, to be honest. You might get a snog from one of the soldier girls, but they're too much hard work. Best sticking to the volunteers.'

The cashier, a Dickensian-Fagan type character, who peered out intermittently from behind an open, large, black cash box, sat behind a wooden desk in an air-conditioned office that smelt of bleach. There was one empty chair facing him and a small filing cabinet against the wall. Superfluous furniture seemed to be lacking everywhere on the kibbutz, more because of an absence of a need or desire for it, than because it was an unaffordable luxury.

I handed over one hundred French francs and he scribbled my name and the amount in shekels on a pink card about the size of a passport, and handed it to me.

'Tankim,' I said as I left, and he peered out from behind the cash box at me, stroking the hairs on his chin.

Charlie went in next and, rather than waiting outside, I walked slowly back towards the dining room. There was a pram parked near the automatic doors, but it was only after I had been standing beside it for a few minutes that I heard a small cry emanating from within. I looked inside and a baby stared up at me. I wondered should I call someone. Had the child been abandoned? The automatic doors opened and a man in his thirties with an Uzi machine gun slung over his shoulder and a bag of sliced white bread in his hand grabbed the pram and pushed it away. How is it that this place is so safe that a baby can be left unattended, free from any danger or harm, and yet a man feels the necessity to carry a gun to protect him from some other perceived danger or harm?

Someone was using the public phone that was mounted on the wall near the entrance to the kitchens. By now, the sense of loneliness I had felt the previous evening had waned, but I still felt a need, and perhaps a puerile duty, to call home. When Charlie arrived, I told him that I was going to call my parents, and that I'd make my own way back to the room. When I finally got through and the collect call charges had been accepted, it was my mother's voice that I heard on the other end. It seemed so very far away and was getting further and further away the more she spoke; it was as if I was falling backwards into the unknown. A terrible homesickness came over me and rushed through my body, almost like a gag reflex to vomit.

I assured her that everything was fine where I was, and that it wasn't the war zone she imagined. 'Not yet anyway,' she hastened to add.

I could picture the dark in Dublin, the beginning of another week in September, every day a little shorter, and every gust of wind a little cooler. A teatime of salads and brown bread, the *Evening Herald* half-read and strewn on the table under empty cups of tea, the music of soap operas followed by the *Nine O'Clock News* on RTÉ One. The cosiness and comfort in the familiarity of family; the presumption of love, unrecognised and unappreciated until far away, and then replaced by a hollow nostalgia that seems hopeless to appease.

After I hung up, I felt both better and worse than before. Outside my room, Ayal and Guy were building a fire inside a small hole that they had dug in the ground. Ayal was lying on his stomach, his head in the hole, blowing on a bunch of dry grass in an effort to ignite the fire. Guy's participation seemed to involve holding a bottle of beer and providing both motivation and instructional advice in between sips. A trail of smoke began to spew out of the grass, and Ayal yelped with excitement. Following further instructions from Guy and further blowing from Ayal, the billowing smoke burst into yellow flames, with Ayal and Guy both taking full credit for its success.

Aengus came out of the room and informed us that he was going to check on where he was working tomorrow. I asked him to check for me too.

'Check mine, will you?' Guy called to him.

'And mine,' Ayal said.

'For fuck's sake,' Aengus grumbled and shuffled off.

In our room, Charlie was mixing together a large basin of flour and water, and dividing it into tennis ball-sized lumps of dough. 'What are you up to?' I asked.

'We're going to make Iraqi flatbread,' he said. 'The girls'll bring over some Nutella and hummus later.'

'Okay,' I said, not knowing what he was talking about.

'Did you manage to call home?' he asked.

'Yeah, everything's okay,' I said.

'Did they tell you to come home?'

'Not really,' I said. 'But it seems like the Kuwaiti invasion is a lot bigger of a deal over there than it is here.'

'Yeah, I know what you mean.'

'They just mostly asked about this place,' I said.

'And what did you tell them?'

'Not much. How do I start explaining this place? I've only been here a day, and I already feel like I've been here a week.'

'How long are you planning on staying?' he asked me.

'Supposed to be till Christmas, but I don't know. Might pack it in and go home earlier.'

'You should try and give the place a month. See how you feel then.'

'Not sure I'm going to last that long to be honest with you, Charlie.'

'Okay, but wait until you see. This place has a knack of sneaking up on you. Then weeks are like days, and it gets harder and harder to leave.'

'We'll see,' I said. 'When are you heading home?'

'Two months ago.'

I laughed.

'Grab one of the beers from the fridge before Aengus drinks them all.'

I took a bottle of Goldstar from the fridge and opened it.

'We take turns filling the fridge with beer,' Charlie said. 'But be warned. Whenever he gets the beer in, the tight fucker turns into an alco overnight and guzzles them down two at a time.'

'Have you phoned home lately?' I asked him.

'No,' he said, but in such a way that I knew it was best to avoid further questioning.

'Can I help you with that?' I asked.

'No, you're all right mate,' he said. 'Go outside, if you want and have your beer.'

I took my cigarettes from the bed and opened the door. 'You never know,' Charlie said smiling. 'Hannah will be over later. A little bit of fraulein might be just what the doctor ordered.'

Twenty feet from our door, the perimeter fence ran straight in both directions. On the other side of the fence was an open plain of flat, hard sand that stretched for miles. In the distance, I could see a mountain range of rocky brown peaks and valleys. The sun was setting to our right, causing huge shadows to creep drowsily across the mountains, like doors closing slowly. There was no wind, but a chalky smell rose up from the ground. I sat on the one-legged sofa and lit a cigarette. Ayal was pacing around the fire adding bigger and bigger pieces of wood.

Guy was still rooted to the same spot, beer in one hand; with the other hand he delivered strategic advice on the best possible positioning of the wood. Markus had joined them and was retrieving rocks from around the area and steadily constructing a small wall around the fire. Guy cracked some joke about the Berlin Wall but nobody laughed.

I stretched out my legs and, leaning back, exhaled a lung-full of smoke into the air above me. It seemed to rest there like a floating white cloud, almost lung-shaped. There was no wind to disperse it – just a nebulous of nicotine moving in slow motion, the darkening sky above it, enduring and static. I was looking down at my chest, rising and falling with each breath, when a sudden urge to call home made me sit up rigidly. But I had just called home. What could I possibly say that wouldn't make me sound pathetic and pitiful? I eventually decided not to do anything, but only after promising myself that I'd call home again tomorrow.

The door of our room opened and Charlie appeared, carrying the tray of dough with a tea towel draped over it.

'For fuck's sake, lads,' he said. 'It's not fucking Guy Fawkes Night.'

Using a stick, he flattened the fire, and then, using the surrounding wall that Markus had built, he placed a wok upside down over the fire.

'Okay,' he said. 'Let's give that a minute.'

Aengus came around the corner and told the others where they were working.

'Joe,' he called over to me. In all my time in the kibbutz, he was the only person who ever called me "Joe". 'Orchards, five a.m.'

'Thanks,' I called back. 'A lie-in so.'

Californian Chad arrived next, carrying a six-pack of beer and a large cassette-radio player, which he plugged into our room. Soon, Bob Dylan's voice was whining into the evening air.

Just as I thought it was going to be an all-male affair, Shir, Hannah and Jenny arrived, carrying more food and drink.

Charlie removed the tea towel from the tray and used it to wipe down the convex side of the wok which was still over the fire. I got off the sofa and went over to him, throwing sneaky glances in Hannah's direction as she laid out some salads, using a chair as a table.

'Do you want to do one?' Charlie asked me.

'What is it?'

'Here, I'll show you,' he said. He took one of the balls and gently kneaded the dough into the shape of a small plate, and then stretching it further outwards at the edges, rotated it in his hands until it was about the width of thick paper.

'Want a go?' he asked and threw the dough onto the back of the wok. He handed me a fresh piece and I caressed it, aware that most of them were observing me closely. Within a few seconds, the dough was the shape of a leather sandal with holes running along it. A pair of hands gently took the dough from me, and I looked up to see Hannah smirking.

'It takes a bit of practise,' she said and taking a fresh piece of dough, she thumped Charlie, who was also laughing.

'Sorry, mate,' he said, and I grinned back at him.

Hannah made another one using the same technique that Charlie had used, while Charlie peeled the edge off the piece he had already placed on the wok and flipped it over onto the other side. He said something to Hannah that I couldn't catch, and she laughed, thumping him again on the arm. He touched the outside of another cooked piece and without him asking her for it, she handed him an empty plate. He nodded at an opened beer just out of his reach; she handed it to him, and he smiled his thanks.

I could hear Aengus complaining to Markus about having to work in the orchards again. 'I heard it's going to be over a hundred degrees tomorrow,' he was telling him, while continuously glancing at Jenny's cleavage. 'It's just getting hotter every fucking day, man. They should have a rule that if it's over a certain temperature, you shouldn't have to work.'

'Did you hear anything about the Swedish group coming?' Markus asked him.

'Aye, they're coming all right,' Aengus said. 'It'll be nice to have a wee bit of talent around here for a change.'

'Oi,' Jenny shouted at him. 'I heard that.'

'No worries there, Jen,' he said. 'I'll always save a wee drop for you.'

'Jesus,' Jenny said. 'I think I'm going to vomit.'

'Pass me that hummus before you do, Jenny,' Charlie said, and she passed a clear plastic tub over to him.

'Here, Joseph,' he said. 'Try some of this.'

He ripped off the plastic top and grabbed a piece of the cooked bread. Scooping up a chalky clay mixture that looked like a cross between baby food and cold porridge, he placed it in his mouth. I looked inside the tub.

'I think she's already vomited into it,' I said. 'What the hell is this?'

'Tasty, that's what it is,' Charlie said. 'Try it.'

I took some of his bread and tasted the smallest bit that I thought I could get away with. It was delicious. In fact, I spent many months after that consuming pots and pots of the stuff.

'How are you settling in?' Hannah was asking me as I was making my way through more hummus.

'Grand, thanks,' I said.

'You sometimes don't look very happy to be here.'

'No, I'm fine,' I said. 'It takes a bit of time to get used to everything, that's all.'

'You worried about a war?'

'No, no, it's just that everything is so new.'

'Maybe the pub tomorrow night will cheer you up,' she said. 'You Irish like the pub, yes.'

'Yes we do,' I said laughing.

'I will buy you a beer tomorrow,' she said. 'They have German beer. This will cheer you up.'

'Thanks, Hannah. That's nice of you.'

'Try to sleep too. It's very important.'

'I will, nurse,' I said. 'I promise.'

She laughed and slapped the side of my arm.

I took Hannah's advice and although it was about eleven o'clock, it looked like nobody was in a rush to leave. I headed back to our room. As I was brushing my teeth, Aengus came in and opened the fridge door.

'I'll give you a shout in the morning if you like,' he said.

'Thanks, Aengus. After this morning, I don't trust my alarm clock.'

'Nay bother,' he said, opening his beer. 'Did Charlie tell you we take turns filling the fridge?'

'Yeah, it's a good idea.'

'But just a wee warning,' he said, lowering his voice. 'Whenever he fills it, he knocks them back like there's no tomorrow.'

I sorted out my clothes for the next day, so at least they'd be ready for the orchards even if I wasn't. Charlie came in just as I was turning out the light.

'All right, mate?' he said grabbing a beer. 'It's my last one, and then I'm heading to bed myself.'

'Okay, goodnight,' I said. 'Hey, Charlie.'

'Yep?'

'I see you and Hannah seem to get on well.'

'Yeah, she's an all right bird,' he said. 'She likes you, anyway.'

'Yeah, she's sound,' I said. 'Tell me, did you... em... did you and her ever, you know?' He turned, and looked out of the window to where the others' incoherent voices could be heard above Bob Dylan.

'Yeah, we did,' he said and turned back to face me. 'When she first got here we hung around for a couple of weeks.'

'Okay,' I said.

'Does that bother you?'

'I don't know. I don't think so.'

'It shouldn't,' he said. 'Life's too fucking short. You're missing out if you let it bother you. You know what I mean?'

'Yeah.'

'You say "yeah",' he said smiling. 'But you still look a little bothered.'

'It's probably from listening to Bob Dylan for the last three hours non-stop,' I said.

He laughed, turned and opened the door to leave.

'Jesus Christ, Chad,' I heard him yelling outside when the door had closed. 'You're killing us with this fucking Bob Dylan marathon.'

I heard Chad replying with a long 'Duuuude' and then launch into a lecture on the god-like status that he and millions of others believe is deservedly bestowed on Dylan.

I turned out the light and lay listening to the cacophony of their voices. I felt different with them than I did with my friends at home; it was as if everything I said and did with these people was new. With friends or people I'd known for years, I was seen in the light of the conversations I'd had years ago or the actions I'd taken up to that moment. But here in the kibbutz, it was all fresh and unknown to me. Here, I suppose, I was new and could be my current self. There was no baggage attached to what I said. I was taken at face value and therefore felt no need to conform to someone else's image of who they thought I was or who they thought I should be. I was seen and accepted for the person I was that day, and it felt good.

Often, at home we'd sit in a pub for hours and whole conversations would revolve around the question, 'do you remember that time when you...?' But here there was no remembering, no past, no history – only the present, with a leaning to the future. Making new memories rather than reliving old ones. And we volunteers felt more of a sense of freedom in that, coupled with an ability to open up. As if our slates had been wiped clean, and we were starting anew, cognisant of the abundance of time and an innate sense that it, Time, was most definitely on our side.

7

We bounced along on a trailer, which was pulled by an old tractor, the driver seemingly blissfully unaware that he had ten passengers hanging on to the wooden sides for dear life. Behind us, it was impossible to see the kibbutz through the clouds of sand and dust billowing from the rear wheels into the sky above us. On the horizon beyond the driver's bobbing head I could see a green border at the base of the mountains – the orchards we were heading for.

Aengus, who had sworn and cursed rhythmically by way of response to every bump, jumped down when we eventually came to an abrupt halt and marched over to the driver, a guy about seventeen years of age.

'Here, Jackie fuckin' Stewart,' he shouted at him. 'You've broken every bone in my fuckin' arse.'

'*Ma?*'(What?) the driver asked.

'My arse. You're driving like a fuckin' lunatic,' he said and walked off, mumbling to himself 'wasting my fuckin' breath.'

Chad, who was wearing an Arab-style headdress, with only his eyes visible, removed the scarf and looked towards the impending sunrise melancholically. He was the type of person who never complained about anything or criticised anyone; he had a constant quizzical expression on his face, as if the whole world and everything in it was a pleasing mystery to him. Of course, this made him instantly attractive to both men and women. Children too seemed to take to him easily, perhaps recognising his child-like essence.

Guy, his head down and looking like he was sleepwalking, dragged his feet lethargically in Aengus's direction. Markus had headphones on and was lip syncing to some 1980s German pop song. He grabbed two Styrofoam containers that I had seen the others filling with water before we left the dining room that morning and followed the rest of the crew - a mixture of Israeli boys and girls whom I didn't know.

'Good morning. Is this your first day in the orchards?' an American voice asked me.

He was a bearded man in his late thirties. When I replied yes, he told me to stick with Chad and Aengus.

The orchard consisted of a few hundred perfectly straight rows of pistachio trees. Like Aengus, I had never seen a pistachio tree, let alone eaten a pistachio nut; neither had I ever worked in any part of the horticultural industry. Needless to say, this fact was of little or no interest to anyone. Volunteers have the least amount of status in a kibbutz; new volunteers considerably less than that. The ranking system is somewhat similar, I imagine, to prisoners in a jail. You work where and when you are told, and you go where and when you are told. The work is, more often than not, arduous and monotonous. Formal introductions to your bosses or to work colleagues are rarely made, as there is always the possibility that after an eight-hour day you may never see each other again. The names of individuals are learned as a result of repeating them again and again over a period of several days. You learn the names of the people working directly beside you, and, as a new worker, you follow their lead. Talk and general chitchat, while not forbidden, is frowned upon. After all, the thinking goes, why use up so much energy talking, and distracting other people's attention when that energy could more appropriately be applied to one's hands and feet for a more useful purpose – working.

This energy distribution theory exerted absolutely no influence whatsoever on Aengus's behaviour.

'I've to work with you and Chad,' I told him.

'You cannae get a much worse job than this,' he assured me.

I had a feeling that no matter what job Aengus was given, it was the 'worse job' you could get. However, on this occasion he wasn't too far off the mark.

Just as the sun peeked above the mountains to begin its laborious day, so too began our laborious day. The first tractor pulled a long conveyer belt down the outside of the first row of trees. Attached to the side of this conveyer belt were two long, green tarpaulins. In the corridor between the first and second row of trees, another tractor, with a bulky, three-pronged claw, moved into position in front of the first tree. Aengus, Chad and I stood alongside one of the tarpaulins. Another two guys and one girl stood beside the other one. By pressing down on a lever, the driver of our tractor released the tarpaulin, and then with us pulling on it, we stretched it out along the ground on either side of the tree. The tree now stood in the centre, with two green plastic blankets lying beneath its branches.

The second tractor manoeuvred the claw onto the trunk of the tree and then shook the living daylights out of it, so that it seemed as if the tree itself would be dragged up by its very roots and flung into the distance. The pistachio tree, quite understandably, had little choice but to give up its fruit. A shower of nuts, leaves, twigs, various species of insects and spiders and layers and layers of dust, descended upon the green blankets on either side of the tree trunk. With another pressing of the lever, we picked up both sides of the tarpaulin and were pulled back under the tree, desperately trying not to scrape our backs on the branches, or worse, lose any of the pistachios. The contents of the tarpaulins were bounced along the conveyer belt into a large plastic square container, to be sorted later.

This process was repeated over and over and over again.

It was approximately twelve months since I had seen the fateful documentary on life in a kibbutz that had first served to act as the spark for this adventure of mine. Now, with my dream fully manifested, I had to admit that it bore only a slight resemblance to my original vision. Instead of looking forward to my body becoming tanned, I feared that my skin would do nothing more than burn, blister and then turn a glowing red. Instead of gently plucking ripe peaches from the branches of trees, I spent my time constantly bent over and being pierced by the thornier lower branches. Instead of looking up at beautiful blonde Swedish babes as they handed me succulent fruit, our fingertips occasionally touching as they smiled down at me, I had to put up with an irritable and irritating, loquacious, garish Scot who groaned and whined like a broken accordion playing 'Bonnie Wee Jeannie McColl'.

And yet, despite all of this, when we packed up our things at around eight o'clock to make our way back to the dining room for breakfast, I felt an enormous sense of well-being and an undeniable feeling of pride at our accomplishments and achievements. Not only had work been done, but also the physical proof in the form of several large containers brimming with pistachio nuts and several more rows of the contents of pillaged and grossly violated trees was clearly visible. Despite Aengus's incessant chatter, my aching back and blistered hands, the dust particles scraping my contact lenses and the scorching sun – despite all of that, I absolutely loved it.

In the dining room, we marched in together like war-weary soldiers returning from the front lines of battle. Our faces and clothes were coated with a thin layer of sandy dust. We filled our plates and trays with well-earned salads and eggs, and we filled our cups with tea and coffee, and we all sat together at the tables in the centre of the room, chatting or reading newspapers. This morning, and every morning, the postmistress placed five copies of the *The Jerusalem Post* into the volunteers' post box. By nine o'clock the pages were stained with egg yolk, ring marks from coffee cups and teacups, and smeared with sporadic blobs of butter. As I ate my own food, I watched the Israelis perform a food preparation ritual with their own salads. They would take each piece in turn – tomato, onion, cucumber, pepper, lettuce – and then chop and dice it until it became hundreds of minute multi-coloured pieces piled up on the plate. The eggs would suffer a similar fate; then olive oil, salt and pepper were added. Each plate had the appearance of a child's painting of an exploded rainbow, and it looked delicious.

When Amit, the American who had spoken to me at the start of the day, discovered I was Irish, he warmed to me and then asked me what had a thousand legs and an IQ of fifty – a Saint Patrick's Day parade, apparently. Like most Americans

I've met, he had a congenial disposition towards full-blooded members of the Irish race. I don't know why this is; I can only conjecture that it has something to do with years of history lessons at school. I imagine that after reading and learning so much about Irish men and women's involvement in the creation of the United States that when they actually meet a real Irish person it's somewhat of a novelty for them.

'Tell me,' I asked him when his sparse supply of crappy Irish jokes had been exhausted. 'What's the difference between a member and a non-member of a kibbutz?' He explained to me that when someone decided they wanted to live and work on the kibbutz and make it their way of life, then they would have to be voted in, in order to become a member. Every other member of the kibbutz would have the right to vote yes or no in favour of the person's membership. This usually only happened after a trial period of at least two years.

He told me that he was originally from California, and that his dream was to one day return to Napa Valley and study winemaking, and then to return and produce wine on the kibbutz. Wine production, he said, had not been attempted in the Negev desert since the time of the Nabateans in the third century BC. I suggested to him that perhaps over that period of nearly two and a half thousand years, no one had been crazy enough to attempt it, let alone succeed.

'Exactly,' he replied with a smile as dry as the Californian chardonnay of which he dreamed.

After breakfast, we bounced our way back to the orchards. Aengus's forecast of an even hotter than normal day appeared to be accurate, and we were all told to drink as much water as we could. Inevitably, the work slowed as we tried to stay in the shade of the trees. If I closed my eyes and put my face to the sun, it was as if an electric heater was blasting away inches from my skin. Just before lunchtime, I saw the orchard bosses, including Amit, having a discussion. After much animated pointing and arm movements, Miguel announced something in Hebrew that made the Israeli workers smile and laugh. Amit walked down to where Aengus, Chad, Guy and I were sitting together under a tree.

'Instead of going back now for lunch,' he said. 'We're going to finish another row and then call it a day, okay?'

'Great,' we all agreed.

'I think by after lunch, it's going to get very hot out here,' Amit said.

'Oh really?' Aengus replied quickly. 'You mean as opposed to the mild spring day we're experiencing at the moment?'

I'm not sure whether it was finishing up an hour early or chronic dehydration, but we were all a little light-headed and in good form as we made our way back to the kibbutz. Personally, I thought there was far too much discussion about far too few options – you could go back to your room where you could read or sleep, or you could go to the pool, where you could also read or sleep. At lunch, in the dining room, Charlie told me he was expecting a big delivery of dry food goods the next day and would ask Rosa to mark me up for the kitchens, so that I could give him a hand. I wasn't quite sure whether he was doing this for my pleasure or for Aengus's annoyance. Back in the room, Aengus was climbing into a pair of shorts and heading over to the pool, so I decided to go with him; half hoping that Hannah would be there.

The surface of the swimming pool shimmered with blue and white light. Around it, on the grass verges, deck chairs and sunloungers had been laid out in the shade of the parasols. A group of soldiers were seated under the olive trees, but there was no sign of any families; it was simply too hot for them. We Westerners, on the other hand, with over twenty years of sun-starved skin to be compensated for, weren't about to allow the slight possibility of melanoma prevent us from soaking up the sun's rays. We slapped on a thin coating of factor five sun lotion (after all, you didn't want to block out too much of the sun) and stretched out on our towels like freshly poured pancake mix onto a frying pan.

The water was cooler than I expected and I was covered in goose bumps. When I got out and dried off, Aengus laughed at how white my skin was. 'You're almost translucent,' he joked. 'I think I can just about see your heart.'

He lay on the grass, his body a dazzling, radioactive red, looking like a Santa Claus decoration that had fallen off a Christmas tree. Hannah came over with Shir to sit with us, and although Shir was arguably the prettier of the two, it was most definitely Hannah, wearing a white bikini, who attracted the most attention from the soldiers. She swam several lengths energetically before raising herself out of the pool, the water gently rolling down her light brown skin, caressing every part of her body as it fell to the ground. Her skin glistened in the sun, her tan further emphasised by the contrasting white bikini. As she bent forward to dry her hair I saw one of the soldiers standing up to get a better view of her.

I felt very lucky as I watched her – even confident that she was going to walk over in my direction. While she was swimming, I had been lying down and reading, or at least pretending to read *Exodus* by Leon Uris. She stood at my feet and splashed some water from her hair on me.

'Hey,' I said. 'Watch the book.'

'Are you really reading?' she asked. 'Or are you just here to look at the pretty girls?'

'Right now, I'm reading. But you never know, maybe later if some pretty girls show up...'

She splashed me again with water, laughing.

I had to hold my hand above my eyes like a military salute as the sun was directly behind her. This only further accentuated her shape, making her look like a vision appearing before me. Aengus, on the other hand, was lying back and scrutinising every inch of her body as if watching a football match on a widescreen television, never once altering his stare as he sipped his beer.

'So, if there's no pretty girl around,' she said. 'Then why aren't you reading now?'

'I can't,' I said. 'You're blocking my light.'

'*Arschloch*,' she laughed. 'Are you implying that I'm fat?'

'No, I'm not implying anything. I'm just saying that the sun is a rather large object for one person to be able to block out.'

She opened her mouth wide, pretending to be thoroughly insulted. 'Did you miss me in the chicken house today?' I asked her.

'No,' she said defiantly.

'Did the chickens miss me?'

'They looked a little sad, now that you mention it. How were the orchards?'

'Great,' I said. 'We even finished up early.'

'Yesterday you're late. Today you finish early. Do you have any plans to do a full day's work?'

'Not if I can help it.'

'You going to the pub tonight?'

'Yes, I have to,' I said.

'You have to? Why?'

''Cause you said you'd buy me beer.'

'I said that I'd buy you one beer.'

'That's good enough,' I told her. 'I get drunk very quickly.'

'So, you are a cheap date?'

'Hey, I never said it was a date, I'm not that easy.'

'You *arschloch*,' she said blushing. 'You would be so lucky.'

'Yes,' I said. 'I would be very lucky.'

She smiled, wrapped the towel around herself and walked back towards her room. Aengus's eyes never once left her as she walked away.

'That is some arse,' he said. 'I'll tell you what, Joe. If I don't get laid some time pretty soon, my aching balls are going to fucking explode.'

With that image of Aengus's exploding testicles in my mind and my own visions of Hannah, I slipped back into the pool to cool off.

That evening, Chad and I were the only two who made it to the dining room for supper. Most of the others were sleeping in preparation for going to the pub. After two months in France experiencing some of the finest cuisine in the world, my palate, and particularly my stomach, were finding these mass-produced meals somewhat of a challenge. So far, anyway, a diet of salads, toast and a strange-looking soft cheese was having little adverse effects on my indigestion.

Chad told me he was from Santa Barbara, a small town about a hundred miles north of Los Angeles. I asked him what he missed most about home, but I would not have been awarded any prizes for guessing his answer.

'Surfing, man,' he said. 'Every sunrise during summer vacation, we'd drive up the coast to Ventura and ride out on our boards, just waiting for the waves. Most mornings, dolphins would swim by. We'd try and float out far enough that we couldn't hear the cars on the freeway. Sometimes we'd just sit there, floating and waiting for hours.'

'Wow,' I said. 'Sounds amazing.'

'It's awesome, man.'

'Too bad we're in the middle of the desert.'

'Depends on your perspective, dude,' he said. 'If you look out the window, this sand could be a beach.'

'But the sea's a hundred miles away.'

'A big beach then,' he laughed.

'A big imagination, you mean.'

'It's all about how you look at it,' he said. 'It's all about perspective.'

'I heard there's surfing up in Haifa, in the north,' I told him. 'You probably wouldn't have to wait too long for a big wave up there.'

'There's a lot to be said for waiting,' he said. 'Besides, there's always a big wave with your name on it on the way. You just have to be ready to ride it when it comes.'

The pub (or the Tea House, as it was called for reasons I was never able to find out) consisted of two white wooden prefabs, each about the size and shape of a large caravan. The building on the left was used as a pub, while the one on the right was a disco, which only opened on Fridays. Between the two was a small concrete courtyard set out with several wooden benches and chairs. Tall palm trees lined both sides of the gravelled entrance; grass surrounded the back of the buildings.

I was told that the buildings had originally been used for housing the security team responsible for guarding the former Prime Minister, David Ben-Gurion, whose house, now a museum, stood close by.

Aengus, Charlie, Markus and Guy were already huddled over four plastic glasses of beer. 'Hey, Joe,' Aengus said as I sat down. 'First-timers always get a round in. It's a tradition.'

'Really?' I asked standing up.

'I did not know this,' Markus said.

Aengus shook his head in disappointment at Markus.

'Never mind,' I said. 'It sounds like a good tradition to start.'

The interior of the pub was both quaint and charming, may both God and Brendan Behan forgive me for using such a description. The walls were made of a dark wood and were decorated with various pictures and posters, mostly drink related – The Ten Stages of Drunkenness, Tuborg lager, Pubs of the World – that sort of thing. Set out on the uncarpeted floor were five round wooden tables, around which were four small wooden stools. In the centre of the room were two long rectangular tables with chairs on either side. The bar itself had a thick wooden countertop, naturally, with a single beer dispenser, and behind the bar were shelves neatly packed with bottles of unfamiliar brands of vodka, whiskey and rum. It was no wonder, I thought, with all the wood used in the construction of this pub, that we were now living in the middle of a desert.

While the Irish are often accused, and rightly so, of using ten words when just one would suffice, the Israelis could equally be accused of thinking that anything more than one word constituted superfluity.

'Goldstar?' the bartender asked me.

'Yeah, please,' I said. 'Is that draught, yeah? How does it come? I mean do you have pints here or is it in litres like in the rest of Europe?

He held up two plastic cups to the tap.

'Third,' he said, holding up the smaller one, and 'half,' as he held up the larger one.

'Okay,' I said. 'I'll have five halves, please. I suppose that makes two and a half.'

'*Ma?*'

'Sorry. Yes, five please. Five halves. *Tankim.*'

He looked at me sideways as he began to pour the golden lager into the cups.

'Do you take it from this?' I asked, holding out my pink card.

He took it, deducted the amount (which I think worked out at less than fifty pence per beer) initialled it, and handed it back to me.

'Thanks,' I said.

He nodded.

'The natives are friendly,' I said, sitting down again and taking a sip from my Goldstar. 'Jesus, that's good stuff.'

'How'd you get on in the orchards today?' Aengus asked me. 'Tough going, eh?'

'Yeah, it was tough at times, all right,' I said. 'But it was okay.'

'Are you with us tomorrow?'

'No,' I said, trying not to look at Charlie. 'I'm in the kitchens.'

'The kitchens?' Aengus repeated and turned to Charlie. 'Are you off tomorrow?'

'No,' Charlie said. 'There's a big delivery coming in, and I need a hand with it.'

'And why didn't you ask for me?'

'I did, mate. But Rosa told me you're too valuable in the orchards.'

'That American from the orchards, Amit, said the same to me,' I told him. 'Indispensable, I think he said.'

'More like indecipherable,' Guy added.

'Amit can go and kiss my white Scottish arse. I'm fucking dying out there,' he grumbled. 'It's no fair. When am I going to get a shot in the kitchens with the girlies?'

'Why don't you buy a few drinks for Jenny tonight?' Charlie suggested.

'Ah, she gets too drunk too quickly,' Aengus said.

'She'd need to be drunk,' Guy said.

'Anyway,' Aengus said. 'I'm no stirring another man's porridge. Especially not yours, Charlie.'

'Jesus, Charlie,' I said. 'Is there anyone on this kibbutz you haven't slept with?'

'Helga Hirsch,' Guy said.

'I wouldn't bet any cash on it,' Aengus said.

'You're a sick fucker,' Charlie said.

'There's some reason you're getting marked up for the kitchen every day, and I plan to find out,' Aengus said.

'Maybe it's because he's doing a good job,' Chad said.

There was a pause before everyone, including Charlie, said 'Nah.'

The door opened and Hannah, Jenny, and Shir came in. Shir went to the bar while Hannah and Jenny came over to sit with us.

'What a surprise to find you all here,' Jenny said.

'I didn't know you were looking for me,' Aengus replied.

'In your dreams,' Jenny said.

'Aye,' Aengus said smiling. 'My wet dreams.'

'Well, that's about as close as you'll ever get,' she replied.

'Oh,' he said to the rest of us. 'I do love a girl that plays hard to get.'

'Impossible to get, in your case.'

'Come and sit down on my knee, Jenny, and I'll show you what a real Scotsman can do.'

'Why?' she asked. 'Can you see one from there?'

Shir came over with three vodkas and coke.

'Starting on the hard stuff already, ladies?' Guy said.

'Hey, Shir,' Charlie said. 'Where's Ayal tonight?'

'How the fuck should I know?' she said, her New York accent stronger than usual. 'I'm not his goddamn mother.'

'Jesus, I'm only asking,' Charlie said.

She went and sat at a table beside us as I took out a cigarette and put it in my mouth.

'No smoking in here, Marlboro Man,' Hannah said, and pulled the cigarette out of my mouth.

'But it's a pub,' I protested.

'A pub made of wood,' she said.

'No smoking in a pub?' I asked. 'You'd never see that in Ireland.'

'I'm going for a smoke outside,' she said picking up her drink. I saw Charlie raise his eyebrows at me as I followed her out the door.

Four high-wattage white bulbs provided the only available light outside but even in the harsh light, Hannah still looked good. I'd never seen her wearing makeup before and I hoped that it was for my benefit. I had come out of my room earlier wearing only a T-shirt and jeans and now felt a chill in the air, which as I sat down opposite her on the bench, caused goosebumps to ripple up my arms. Mind you, it most likely also had something to do with the excitement, anticipation and nervousness that forever resulted from meeting someone new. I lit my cigarette, then lit hers, and sipped my beer, which now seemed much colder than it had earlier.

'It's cold,' I said to her shivering slightly.

'Of course it's cold,' she said. 'It's the desert. Didn't you study geography in school?'

'I never went to school,' I said.

'No?' she asked. 'Were you raised by wolves in Ireland?'

'Cats actually.'

'Cats?' she laughed. 'My mother had two pet cats. They were always fighting and shitting everywhere. I hate cats.'

'You should try living with them,' I said

I sipped on my beer, and she sipped on hers. There was a slight uneasiness for a moment, as if we were both thinking of something to say.

'How's your book?' she asked.

'What book?'

'The *Exodus* book.'

'It's okay. Have you read it?' I asked.

'No, but I have never seen a non-Jewish person reading this book.'

'Well, how do you know I'm not Jewish?'

'I know,' she said.

'Have you been spying on me in the shower?'

'No, *arschloch*.'

'So how do you know?' I asked.

'Because I have been asked many times here if I am Jewish but never by non-Jewish people, and you have not asked me,' she explained.

'So are you Jewish?' I asked.

'No,' she laughed.

'So why are you here?'

'Why are you here?'

'I asked you first,' I said.

'My grandfather was Jewish. He disappeared in 1938 when my mother was two years old,' she said.

'Disappeared?'

'The Nazis were in power, and that is what happened. People disappeared.'

'And your grandmother?' I asked.

'After the war started, she hid with my mother in the basement of a neighbour's house. For four years they never left the basement. Then in 1943 there was an air raid, and a bomb killed everyone in the house except my mother.'

'And what happened to her?'

'She was adopted by another neighbour,' she said.

'Wow, that's an amazing story,' I said. 'So do you have family in Israel?'

'That's why I came to check,' she said. 'My mother said that she remembers her mother saying that my grandfather had run away to Israel. I thought it might be possible that he had maybe joined the army here, or even started a new family.'

'And did you find anything?'

'*Nicht*,' she said and lit another cigarette.

'I'm sorry,' I said.

'For what?'

'I don't know. It's just a sad story.'

'Yes, but there were tens of millions of sad stories at that time. It is just another one.'

I took another mouthful from my beer and watched her face as she inhaled the cigarette.

'And what about you?' she finally asked me.

'What about me?'

'Why are you here?'

'The cats,' I said.

'The cats?'

'They threw me out.' We spent the remainder of the night drinking, smoking and talking – the foundation of any good relationship – only stopping when necessary to order more beer or to piss it out. For her, the bathroom consisted of a single cubicle attached to the end of the pub. For me, it was a case of any tree or bush, preferably not attached to the pub. Everyone seemed aware that Hannah and I had our own thing going on, and they pretty much left us alone. I was surprised when Charlie and Aengus came up to me and said that the pub was closing and they were heading back to the room. Within a few minutes, the pub and all the tables outside emptied. The lights were turned off inside, and the bartender came outside and locked the door. He looked surprised to see us still there.

'You want more beer?' he asked.

'No thanks,' I said. 'Unless you do, Hannah.'

'No, I'm fine, thanks,' she said.

'Before go home,' he said pointing at the light switch outside the door. 'You shut light here, okay?'

'Okay, *tankim*,' I said.

He looked at me strangely.

'*Lila tov*,' he said.

'*Lila tov*,' Hannah said.

'Lily dove,' I said.

He threw his leg over his bicycle and peddled off, whistling to himself. We listened to him whistling as he cycled up the road.

'What did you say to him?' Hannah asked me.

'Lily dove. Is that wrong?'

'It's *lila tov*. *Lila* is night and *tov* is good,' she explained. 'But before that. What did you say?'

'*Tankim.*'

'What's *tankim* mean?'

'What's *tankim*? It's thanks,' I said. 'Didn't you know that?'

'You mean thank you?'

'Yeah, thank you or thanks.'

'Thanks is *toda*,' she said.

'So what the fuck am I saying?'

'I think you're saying tanks.'

'Thanks?'

'No,' she said. 'Tanks. As in army tanks. Sherman tanks.'

'So why did Eli tell me it was *tankim*?' I asked.

'I think it's your Irish accent. When you say thanks, it sounds like tanks.'

'Oh shit,' I said. 'I've been saying *tankim* to everyone. They probably think I'm a lunatic.'

She burst out laughing. 'A lunatic?' she said. 'You're lucky they didn't shoot you.'

'On that note,' I said laughing, and stood up to leave.

She put out her cigarette.

'*Scheisse*,' she said looking at her watch. 'I'm up for work in five hours.'

'Yes, you're right,' I said. 'We should get to bed.'

'What?'

'I mean... I'm up early also... I didn't mean... First day in the kitchen. We both need sleep.'

'Let's go,' she said.

We walked slowly together up the gravelled entrance and out onto the quiet road that led back to the rooms, both of us in our own thoughts.

'Oh shit, the lights,' I said and ran back to the pub to switch them off.

When I got back to her, she had her arms wrapped around herself, waiting for me.

'I'm cold,' she said.

Instinctively, I placed my arms around her and almost without realising it, her mouth was against mine. The smell of her hair and perfume warmed me from the inside as her hands found their way inside my shirt, and her open palms caressed my back. I took this as permission to do the same and felt the smooth, hot skin of her back before sliding my hand to her front. She rewarded my audacity with her tongue, and I pressed closer into her as her nails dug gently into my back. She slipped one hand from my back and down my side and towards my stomach, boldly letting her hand fall lower and lower.

Even with my closed eyes, I felt the brightness of the sudden light on my face. We both separated from each other and turned to see six headlights from a jeep beaming at us. We both raised our hands to protect our eyes and moved out of the way to allow the jeep to pass. As it slowed down, I could see that it was David on security duty.

He lowered his window, a big smile on his face.

'Hi, David,' I said, a little embarrassed as if caught with a girl by my dad. Hannah fixed herself behind me.

'Get a room, you guys,' he smiled.

'We were just going to bed now,' I told him.

'I don't doubt that, my brother.'

'No, I mean, our own beds. We were just...'

'Hey, I'm just messing with you, kid,' he said. 'Is the pub closed?'

'Yeah, about twenty minutes ago.'

'Okay,' he said, putting the jeep into gear. 'Have a safe night, you guys.'

'Ok, thanks,' I said.

'*Tankim,*' Hannah said and elbowed me in the side.

When he had driven off, we both smiled at each other. I took her hand and put my arm around her, and we walked side by side back to our rooms, our bodies gently bumping off each other as we moved.

8

When we reminisce, we can easily recall the major events and episodes in our lives that prove to be of monumental significance – the births, the deaths, the marriages. We tend to forget about the other incidents and deeds of a lesser significance – the answering of a phone, the turning of a corner, the chance encounter. And yet, it is these very commonplace acts, made almost always unconsciously, that are the real determinants of our path through life. It is the careless turning of a card, the indifferent rolling of the dice, the moving one space forward of a pawn. These smaller steps are covert catalysts that bounce us off in a different direction and lead us to truly life-changing experiences. Acts performed nonchalantly hundreds, or possibly thousands, of times, but every now and then, one of these seemingly ordinary acts turns out to be the seed of something extraordinary. Then, as naturally and as permanently as a bend in a river, we are changed forever.

And so it was, on that Wednesday morning, as I sat sipping my tea in the dining room, my mouth dusty dry from a night of drinking and smoking, that such an insignificant and yet life-changing event happened to me. For reasons of preferred anonymity, I will call her M.

Perhaps if I had not been sitting there at that moment; perhaps if I had been assigned to work in the orchards for that day; perhaps if the woman in Tel Aviv had chosen a completely different kibbutz for me; or perhaps it was predetermined; perhaps there is something in fate and destiny. Or perhaps not.

I raised the cup to my mouth just as she turned and walked towards the water tap in front of me. Time slowed and a silence descended over me. I could feel my heart ache and thump harder in my chest. My eyes devoured her every movement, her every expression. Someone passed her and said hello and she smiled at them and the room seemed to brighten. She turned her demure face towards them to reveal a profile of classical symmetry. Another person asked her a question and she responded in Hebrew, the normally harsh and guttural-sounding language elevated to that of a chiming bell.

I had arrived, you must remember, after spending two full months in the South of France where attractive, even stunning, girls and women are as commonplace as baguettes in a boulangerie. In Israel, the bar had been raised even higher by a mixture of Eastern, Western, Russian and indigenous girls of exquisite beauty. And yet, here among that aesthetic altitude, an even higher peak of perfection had been reached. M was indisputably and quite obviously the most beautiful girl I had ever seen. She stood, a few feet away from me, deliriously oblivious to my very existence.

She walked towards me and then turned into the kitchen. I placed my cup back on the table, my mouth and throat drier than ever, my hand slightly shaking.

Charlie was coming out of the kitchen and smiled at her as he passed.

'I bet you don't see too many like her in Dublin,' he said, standing in front of me.

'Charlie, you don't see too many like her anywhere,' I said.

'How did you get on with Hannah last night?' he asked.

I wish that I could tell you that it was with irony, or humour or even cruelty that I replied to Charlie with, 'who?' I suddenly realised that my desire for Hannah had deflated quicker than the pricking of a balloon and had been washed away like a tidal wave crashing down onto a pond.

'Oh, it's like that, is it?' he asked.

I didn't reply.

'Come on then, I'll give you the tour.'

The kitchen was divided into two sections, a dry area and a wet area. Both were an expanse of spotless, stainless steel, which sparkled in the sunlight that was pouring in through the windows. Tables, benches, utensils, and several metallic machines used for chopping, peeling and frying stood poised and ready for action. The dry section, the larger area, held the cookers, fryers and two huge ovens the size of a vending machine. The wet area held mostly tables, chopping and dicing machines, and a walk-in fridge that was linked to a smaller freezer inside.

Various bright-coloured buckets were dotted around the floor. On each of the bucket lids was a length of white masking tape denoting its contents, hand-written in both Hebrew and English. 'Potatoes' spelt without the 'e'. 'Eggs' with only one 'g', 'yogurt' surprisingly spelt correctly, and 'vegetable soap'. (Although, in fairness, I'd tasted the soup once, and that misnomer could be forgiven.) Outside was another small work area that overlooked a courtyard for delivery trucks; this area contained a pair of massive green bins. Beyond that was a small road running alongside several rows of olive trees. At the end of this area was another freezer about the shape and size of a forty-foot shipping container.

I had spotted M near the far end of the kitchen where she was in the process of peeling and chopping her way through a line of onion-filled buckets. Outside, Charlie had spread out on the ground several round basins, and had loaded these basins with industrial-sized packets of frozen fish from South America. He was using a hose to fill the metal basins with water before placing them in direct sunlight so as to speed up the defrosting process. I asked him about M, desperate for any information.

'Not too sure, mate' he said.

'Is she one of the soldiers?' I asked.

'No, she only works here once a week on Wednesdays. She lives here.'

'What? With a boyfriend or something?'

'No, with her family,' he said. 'She was studying in France for the last year.'

'Really? What part?'

'How the fuck should I know? But to be honest with you, you're wasting your time, mate.'

'Why, has she a boyfriend?'

'I don't know, but it's not that,' he said. 'It's just not a common thing, you know, a volunteer going out with one of the daughters of the kibbutz. I told you that already. It just doesn't happen that often.'

'But it has happened, right?'

'Jesus, listen to you,' he said. 'What happened to Hannah? You were all over each other last night, and now you're already chasing someone else?'

I looked over to where M stood, her head facing down, concentrating on her work. Every time I looked at her, my heart would start pounding faster. Golda, a middle-aged woman, and the boss of the kitchen, opened the clear plastic door and stuck her head out.'

'Charlie,' she called.

'Coming now, Golda,' Charlie called back.

He slapped me on the back.

'Look, you do what you want,' he continued. 'But if I were you, I'd stick with Hannah. We're only going to be here for a short time, and you're going to waste that time chasing a hopeless cause. I've never even seen her down the pub, so I don't think she's eighteen yet.'

'Shit, really,' I said. 'She's only seventeen? She looks older.'

'They always do here,' he said. 'Anyway, from what I've heard, the embassies are going to advise all of us to leave soon.'

'Why?'

'Why? Why the fuck do you think?' he asked, and then whispered to me, but not before looking over his shoulder. 'Cause there's a chance that Israel is going to get bombed to fuck in the next couple of months. That's why.'

'That's not going to happen,' I said.

'Oh yeah? And how do you know that?'

I didn't answer him.

'Exactly,' he said. 'You don't know. No one knows. But what I do know is that there's a nuclear base in Dimona about twenty miles from here and if that gets a direct hit...'

'Charlie, please,' Golda called to him again.

'Sorry, coming now,' he said, and then turned back and stared at me.

I looked over at M again. I looked back at Charlie. I hadn't noticed how blue his eyes were before. I nodded at him and then smiled.

'Fuck it,' I said, and then turned and walked towards M.

'By the way,' he called after me.

I turned around to face him.

'I don't think she even speaks English,' he said smiling.

She kept her head down as I opened the door beside her.

'*Bonjour,*' I said. She turned her head to face me and looked me straight in the eye.

'*Bonjour,*' she replied smiling. I could feel my chest contracting around my heart, forcing it to beat faster and faster.

'*Tu es triste, ou c'est les onignons qui te font pleurer?*' I asked.

'*Les oignons,*' she laughed.

'*Tu es sure? Parce que j'ai une histoire drôle, si c'est ne pas les oignons…*' I said.

'*Oui, oui, je suis sure. Merci,*' she said.

Silence. Shit, I should have thought this through a bit more. She returned to chopping the onions. Think, you idiot, think.

'*Es tu Francais?*' she asked.

Saved.

'*Non, Irlandais.*'

'*Ils parlent Francais en Irlande?*'

'*Non, nous parlons Anglais.*'

'So, I can to speak in English?' she asked.

'Sure,' I said. 'No problem.'

'I need to start to practise my English.'

'Good,' I said. 'I don't know much more French.'

'Why do you not to speak Irish in Ireland?'

'Christ, that's a long story. But if I told you that one, then I'd really have you crying over your onions.'

'*Comment?*' she asked.

'It's a long story,' I said, stretching my hands apart, trying to translate the 'long'. '*Une histoire longue.*'

'Oh,' she said.

'Maybe some other time I can tell you?' I asked.

'Some other...?' she asked.

'Another time,' I said. 'Now I need to work.'

'Yes, and I need to...' She mimed the action of her chopping.

'Chop,' I said.

'Chop?' she said.

I nodded.

'Chop, chop, chop,' she said smiling.

'Exactly. I need to chop chop too,' I said laughing and turning away. 'What's your name?

'M,' she said.

'M,' I repeated. 'I'm Joseph.' She didn't repeat my name but instead nodded and held my eye contact for a few seconds. Then she bent her head, returning to her work, but not before I noticed the dark colouring of a blush creeping across her face.

By lunchtime, contrary to Charlie's prediction, things were going quite well between M and I. We had spoken, albeit briefly, a few times, shared a couple of silly jokes, and had even done the old faithful 'splashing each other playfully with water' routine. Amazingly, she grew more and more beautiful as the day went on and as I, simultaneously, grew more and more fond of her. A few times, I noticed one or two of the women who worked in the kitchens looking at us with an interest that seemed a little foreboding. It was only as a result of glances out of the corner of my eyes that I noticed them at all because as soon I turned to face them, they quickly turned away.

On one occasion, Golda looked straight at M while we were talking and M turned away from me and returned to her work. I thought at first that this was merely a visual reprimand from the boss, but there was more to it than that. There was an edge to her look. Something more than mere disapproval of our work standards – more of a general disapproval. As if we were doing something morally wrong, something sinister. I wondered if it was a Jewish thing. Was our friendliness in their eyes not seen as, well, kosher? Of course we only chatted after that whenever Golda was out of sight. I didn't really give the issue much further thought, although Golda's look proved disheartening enough to prevent me from asking M if she'd like to meet up later in the day.

It didn't prevent me, however, from wishing that my time in the kitchens would never end. Aengus was right, it was a handy job, but I would have happily gone back to the chicken house and sat looking down a chicken's arse all day if I knew that M was also going to be within my view. And so, when Charlie called me to lunch, I sulked my way out to the dining room, knowing that time was passing, and that my day in the kitchen was coming to an end. Would I not now see M for another week? Worse, I probably wouldn't even be put to work in the kitchens next week. My despondency quickly turned to outright panic when I saw Hannah approaching me, arms outstretched.

Bollox, I thought.

'How's my little kitchen boy today?' she said wrapping her arms around me and kissing me on the mouth.

I held her waist with my two hands and pulled back slightly from her kiss.

'What's wrong?' she asked a little hurt.

'Nothing,' I said. 'It's just...'

'Ah,' she smiled. 'Is my little kitchen boy shy?'

'Yes, that's it,' I said, pushing her further away from me, now that she'd given me an excuse to.

'Okay, then,' she said and let go of me. 'See you later.'

As I lowered my arms to release her, she pounced back and planted a huge kiss on my mouth. With my eyes open, I could see the first few tables where people were sitting and eating. They were all focused on their lunches or on each other, ignoring us, except for one stern face, chewing on her food like a cow chewing its cud. My eyes met Golda's, her fork poised just below her mouth as she chewed and chewed, and stared and stared.

Hannah finally released me and trotted off with Shir down the stairs. I watched them descend just as I saw M walking out of the kitchens and taking a tray.

'*Bon appetit*,' she said, and I managed a smile in return.

Although I never looked in Golda's direction while I queued for my food and deliberately kept my face pointed at anything and everything except Golda, I could still see, out of the corner of my eyes, her mouth chewing slowly and sideways, her glare following me around the room like the picture of the Sacred Heart that my grandmother used to have hanging in her sitting room.

After lunch, the truck that Charlie had promised would be arriving finally turned up, and we spent the next two hours unloading it into the storeroom below – heavy white bags of flour, sugar and rice, and shiny tins of jams, olives and gherkins. The storeroom was located underneath the kitchen stairs, so we had to carry every item from the truck and place it in the room. It was no wonder Charlie had asked for an extra pair of hands. For the hour and a half that it took us to unload the truck, the driver sat under the shade of an olive tree drinking coffee and smoking. I didn't mind that so much, but I didn't understand why he had to stretch himself out only a few feet from where we worked. He just lay there for the entire time watching us. When Charlie realised that the driver didn't speak a word of English, he started verbally abusing him, smiling all the while.

'You're such a lazy prick, I bet you wear a nappy.'

'You like looking at our arses while we work, don't you?'

'I bet your dick is about the same shape and size as one of these olives.'

When the truck finally drove away, we went back upstairs to find that the kitchen was almost back to the same condition it had been in when I first arrived that morning. Charlie told me that every inch of every piece of equipment was washed and scrubbed once a day, as was every corner of the dining room. The staff were finishing up, an Israeli pop song was playing, and everyone was in a jovial mood as they washed the floor with soap and then rinsed it with water.

M was washing down the table where she had been working for most of the day. 'You're not working here tomorrow?' I asked her.

'No,' she said. 'Tomorrow I study. And you?'

'I don't know. Wherever they put me.'

'You not work here?'

'Maybe,' I said. 'Why? Will you come visit me?'

'No,' she laughed.

I grabbed the brush from her hand. 'Hey,' she said. 'I need to finish.'

'So promise me you'll visit me,' I said, holding the brush out of her reach.

'Okay, I promise,' she said, and as I handed her back the brush, she flicked the water back at me.

I skipped down the stairs of the dining room and found Aengus and Guy on their funereal march back from the orchards.

'Look at that, Guy,' Aengus said nodding towards me. 'It's a real Irish jig for you.'

I smiled back at him.

'Enjoying the kitchens, I see,' he said.

'Yeah, they're handy all right,' I replied. 'What news from the orchards?'

'Here's a bit of news for you. It's your turn to fill the fridge and the Colbo's open.'

'Lead the way so,' I told him.

The Colbo was a small shop that opened for a couple of hours every day, although never at the same time. Some days it would be first thing in the morning and then other days, last thing at night. I think it chose its opening hours based on an ancient astrological equation translated from the Dead Sea Scrolls. I never quite managed to figure out what day and when, so whenever it was open, it was always best to ensure you topped up on supplies of cigarettes and beer.

The shop itself was always deliciously air conditioned and stocked mostly with toiletries, confectionery and drinks. The kids bought chocolate and Coca-Cola, and the adults bought cigarettes and beer; after that, each shuffled off to their respective corners for twenty minutes of solitary sensory gratification.

The three of us left the shop carrying a case of beer each, a bag filled with our weekly allocation of free cigarettes and each of us sucking on ice cream. We plodded our way back to the room, the sun exerting a heaviness on us that forced us to drag our feet. Both of them fired questions at me about Hannah, which I tried my best to deflect.

After we had filled the fridge, we sat outside contemplating the desert, drinking our beers, smoking our cigarettes and talking our bullshit. After a couple of beers, Guy and Aengus went off to their rooms for a siesta; I stayed outside drinking, smoking and contemplating. I heard footsteps and turned to see Charlie holding a bag full of cigarettes and beer. He was smiling a mischievous smile that made me sit up a little.

'How are you?' he asked.

'Great,' I said.

'And what did you think of the kitchen?' he asked, sitting down beside me.

'Not a bad job.'

'Good, good. And what did you think of M? I see you two got on rather well.'

'Yeah, she's pretty amazing,' I said.

'And amazingly pretty,' he replied.

'What's wrong?' I asked.

'What do you mean?'

'Come on. Did she say something to you?'

'To me? No,' he said.

'So what is it?'

'Well, I don't think Golda was too impressed.'

'Golda? Fuck Golda,' I said with a lot more venom than I had intended. 'It's none of her business what M and I do.'

'Did you know that Golda's daughter studies with M?' he asked.

'So?'

'And they're close friends.'

'Great,' I said sipping my beer. 'Maybe you could ask her daughter out and we'll do a double date. Take them both to the pub or into Beersheba. See how she likes that.'

'No,' he laughed. 'I don't think that's going to happen.'

'Well, you don't have to, but I'm going to.'

'Okay, but probably best not to do it on a school night.'

'What do you mean?'

'I mean they're both still at school,' he said.

'School? You mean college,' I said.

'No, I mean school.'

I looked at him not understanding what he was talking about.

'Mate, she's fifteen years of age.'

An hour later and with both Charlie and Aengus asleep, I tried to read *Exodus* by the beams of sunlight streaming through the window. After re-reading the same paragraph for ten minutes, I threw the book on the floor.

Fifteen years of age. Christ, what a nightmare. I thought of my younger sister. She had just turned fifteen. She was just a child. A kid. As were all her friends. The thoughts of me going out with one of them. Of even being attracted to one of them. What a joke. And yet when I thought of M, I couldn't come close to comparing her with any of them. I felt as if I'd been shown a cage full of golden treasures, and then Charlie had come along and locked the door shut on me. My thoughts of leaving the kibbutz sooner than I'd originally planned returned to me like floodwater bursting through a dam. A five-year difference would be fine if I were twenty four. But fifteen was still fifteen. What if I had actually asked her out? Christ, what if she had said yes? No wonder those old crones in the kitchen were giving me the evil eye. I was lucky they hadn't tried to kick me out of the kibbutz right there and then.

So what to do? Nothing. That's what I decided. To completely forget about her and do absolutely nothing.

But it was just so... so... ah, fuck, I thought, and reached for my book again.

Eventually, I nodded off at some point but was woken by the sound of knocking on the door. I opened my eyes slowly, but the room was in darkness now. Again, a knock, only louder this time and with an impatience to it. I heard the door opening with a creak, but it was dark outside so no light came in. I could make out from the shadowy outline that it was Hannah, and I closed my eyes again.

'Hallo?' she said.

Like a child pretending to his parents that he was asleep, I kept my eyes closed. I could hear her breathing and then eventually turning and going out again. I opened my eyes as she closed the door. The noise of the door closing caused both Charlie and Aengus to stir. Charlie stretched out and looked over at me.

'What time is it?' he asked.

I looked at my watch. 'Seven.'

He yawned loudly causing Aengus to turn over on his side.

'Let's go get something to eat,' he said.

'I think I'll stay here,' I said.

'Why?'

I shrugged.

'You avoiding Hannah?' he asked. Charlie was very sharp.

'I'll talk to her tomorrow,' I said. 'I just don't want to talk to her now, that's all.'

'Okay, I'll bring you back something,' he said. 'Here, Scottie. We're going for something to eat.'

Aengus groaned and pulled the blankets up closer to his neck. Charlie got out of bed and scratched his underpantsed arse, walking towards Aengus.

'Beam me up Scottie,' he yelled, a few inches from his head.

'Fuck you,' Aengus moaned back.

They left, they ate, I read and they returned. Aengus came in first, and then Charlie, closely followed by Hannah.

'I was just telling Hannah,' Charlie blurted out, winking at me. 'I was just telling her that you weren't feeling too well.'

I coughed a couple of times.

'Pains in your stomach, I was saying,' he said.

I stopped coughing and began appropriately rubbing my stomach.

'Are you okay, Joseph?' Hannah asked.

'It's just a cramp,' I said.

'Will I ask Hadar to get you a doctor?'

'No, no,' I said. 'I'll be fine, I'm sure.'

'You shouldn't go to work tomorrow,' she suggested.

'Where am I working?' I asked.

'The dishwater,' Aengus said but in a tone that might better have suited "The Abyss of Hell".

'It's probably best if I go,' I said. 'I don't want to be calling in sick on my first week.'

'Can I get you anything?' she asked.

'No, thanks. Even the thoughts of food would make me vomit.'

'I was going to go for a night walk in the desert looking for some night creatures with Shir and Jenny, but I'll tell them I'm not going.'

'The only night creature you'll see out there is Jenny,' Aengus added. 'A right man-eater if ever there was one.'

'No no,' I blurted out. 'You go. I probably just need to sleep a little. I'll be fine.'

'Are you sure? I don't mind staying here with you.'

'That's so sweet of you, Hannah,' I said. 'But I'd hate to ruin your night as well.'

'Okay,' she said. 'I'll check in on you when we come back.'

'Thank you.'

She leaned down and kissed me on the mouth for several seconds and then let go.

'Enjoy yourself,' I groaned.

She turned and smiled sympathetically at me. As she closed the door behind her, Charlie threw the bag of food on my bed.

'Sorry about that, mate,' Charlie said. 'She insisted on coming in.'

'You're grand,' I said. 'Sorry to get you involved in my crap.'

'How are you getting on with that book?'

'It's tough going,' I said. 'Seems like it's taking me forever.'

'I'm going to the English library in a few minutes if you want to come along?'

'Library? Great.'

'You coming, Aengus?'

'Aye, let's go,' he said.

'Can we wait a minute or two till we hear the girls leave?' I asked.

We sat in relative silence until we heard the three girls' chatter as they opened and closed doors and then listened to their chitchat gradually abate as they walked up the road.

'Night creatures,' Aengus said. 'They'll probably get eaten alive by a fucking hyena or something.'

'Are you joking me? Listen to the noise of them,' Charlie added. 'They'll scare off every animal within ten miles.'

The English library was located in the bomb shelter under the dining room. Rows and rows of colourful used books lined up against the civil servant-grey concrete walls. I love second-hand books; the musty smell of the printed words on yellowed paper; the softness of the pages, the result of being seduced by hundreds of hands over a period of years and years; the soothing sound as the pages are flicked through, chapter by chapter; the books' stoical patience as they sit and wait for their next benefactor to play with them.

There was an organised disorder to the books on the shelves as I explored the various sections of fiction, non-fiction, war books (didn't see a peace section), history, poetry etc. I smiled whenever I came across an Irish writer, and reached out to gently touch the book binding – Wilde, Yeats, Stoker, and of course Joyce. Well, it could hardly have been called a library without including him, could it?

Charlie held up the paperback cover of a book – *Catch-22* by Joseph Heller.

'Did you ever read this?' he asked.

'No,' I said. 'I saw the film though.'

He scoffed at this and placed it firmly in my hands.

I sat on the stairs and read the first page and knew that I would love it. Charlie and Aengus were still browsing, cocooned in their private world of words, as libraries give you permission to be.

'I'll see you back at the room,' I said to Charlie when I'd checked out the book, and he nodded.

I climbed the concrete stairs out of the bomb shelter-cum-library and stood for a minute breathing in the viscous night air. It was about nine o'clock, and the thoughts of going back to my room didn't appeal to me so I wandered down a path in the opposite direction. The dark green lawns, like carpets, stretched out on either side. A dormant playground awaited now-snoozing children and the return of the sun. Tall street lamps shone down and coloured the tops of the trees, painting their leaves orange and white. A door slammed shut, and someone called out, 'Roni Roni,' and then the door opened and closed again. A dog appeared from a smaller path, its paws slapping the concrete as it crossed aimlessly in front of me.

I turned right and walked along the main road that ran through the centre of the kibbutz. I saw a group of people ahead, gathered in front of a large yellow forklift with the word 'Manitou' written on the side. The two round white headlights of the Manitou illuminated the group of about ten people, mostly guys, as they pushed and grappled each other to gain a better position. They shouted in deep yet adolescent voices, and jostled each other in an animated yet amiable way. I slowed my pace to see what they were doing, unsure how they would react to my presence. Fortunately, they just ignored me so I stood on a raised sewer to look over their heads.

On the pointed tip of each of the forks, tied upside down by its feet, dangled a flapping and seriously bad-tempered chicken. The forks were raised to such a height that the two chickens' bodies were about level with the heads of the teenagers. Two volunteers (or victims) stepped forward from the crowd and stood on either side of each chicken, encouraged by slaps on their backs and by the calling of their names. The one nearest to me was a heavy-set guy in his mid-teens with a round mound of curly hair that covered most of his face. The second guy was more athletic, and I thought that whatever they were about to do, the smart money was on him. Amid chorused calls of *'muchanim'* and *'yalla, yalla'* the group slowly inched backwards and formed a semi-circle around the two guys and their two chickens. It was only then that I saw the large knives in each of their hands.

They simultaneously grabbed hold of the chickens' heads and pulled them downwards, exposing their long red necks. They then gently placed the blades against the necks and turned to face the group. A silence fell upon the crowd and even the chickens stopped flapping in an apparent resignation to their fate.

'*Sa*,' a voice called out, and both boys snapped their attention back to the chickens and cut into the necks with ruthless determination. The boys' faces contorted with exertion as their arms and hands shot from side to side, almost blurred with the speed. Excited roars from the audience encouraged them on, and they waved their arms in a frenzy that bordered on hysteria. I was surprised at how taken aback I was when the first chicken's head popped off in the hand of the winner. What the hell was I expecting would happen? Rather than raise his bloodied knife in the air, proclaim his victory and be swarmed with a congratulatory crowd, he turned and ran away. So too did the crowd. Then I realised what they were betting on and more importantly what was at stake for the loser.

The decapitated chicken swung violently from side to side, and up and down, swaying and spewing and spraying streams of blood from its open neck. Although I'm quite sure that both chickens would have contested who the real losers in this little foursome were, the perceived losing contender, obviously prohibited from leaving until his task was complete, was showered with the gooey and warm blood that splattered his face, body and unruly hair. The white headlights of the Manitou turned red as they too were splashed, transforming the eerie setting into what could easily have been a scene from a David Lynch film.

Eventually, the head came off and the losing contender, with chicken head in hand, ran to the side before a further onslaught of blood drenched the ground and transformed what was left of the remaining white light into bright red. I stepped off the sewer and left them to their babbling, their boasting and their two bloodied and limp dead birds.

I turned right again and passed some smaller chalets that were built in parallel rows, divided by lengths of grass and bushes. A tall, thick hedge on my right blocked my view, and when I reached the end of the path, I found myself back in front of the dining room. The automatic glass doors opened. I could see that the lights were turned off in the dining room upstairs but I continued climbing the steps, as I was still not ready to return to our room. I touched the enormous water boiler, and it was still quite hot. Taking a cup I spooned in some hot chocolate powder and sugar, and then filled it with the warm water. I sat at the first table, tempted to light a cigarette, but decided against it.

Thoughts of M had been with me all evening, almost like a physical presence following me around. What made me think of her in this way? What was so special or different about her?

I could hear the crickets through the open windows, but the stillness in the dark dining room was palpable. I listened to myself breathing, and tried to think of anything except M. I even tried to conjure up feelings for Hannah, but with little success. Like holding the needle of a compass away from pointing north, and then letting go, so too my thoughts always came back to M, even without my being aware of it. I suppose I must have had a sort of infatuation for her; her physical beauty had undoubtedly captured my attention. Looking back now, this marked the first time in my life that I actually fell in love.

I sipped my hot chocolate, wishing it were something stronger, and placed it back on the table. The noise of it touching the table echoed through the dining room, and then stillness again, and then the crickets returned, and then so too did my thoughts of M.

9

The next time I saw M was the following morning while I was drinking coffee and sitting in the dining room in the same chair as the previous night, and waiting for my shift to start as the kibbutz's newly appointed dishwasher. As soon as I saw her, my heart started to race, and I turned my attention downwards and into the darkness of the coffee. When I dared to look over in her direction, she was looking at me and she waved. I smiled back as non-committal a smile as I could muster.

I was waiting for a guy named Itai. He was to spend time with me explaining the machine and giving me a general rundown of the dos and don'ts. He was late. We were supposed to have started at seven, and it was already twenty past. Tamar, the woman in charge of the dining room, had already introduced herself. She spoke good English and smiled and laughed easily. She also frowned and shouted just as quickly. I wasn't sure whether I should be complacent with her or cower from her.

'Who is it that you are supposed to meet?' she eventually asked, her patience obviously wearing out.

'I think it's Itai,' I said. She swore in Hebrew under her breath and marched off.

A stooped figure in a red baseball cap walked in. He had his head hung low. The peak of his cap covered most of his face, so that I could only make out a protruding stubbled chin. He took a cup from the tray and made his way to the water boiler. As he was spooning in the third sugar into his coffee, I saw Tamar notice him, and like a cat spotting a mouse, she sprang over. This was Itai.

She spewed out her unhappiness all over the side of his face in a barrage of barely concealed aggression. He stirred his coffee slowly, sipped it, and then added another spoonful of sugar. As she continued her tirade of angry questions, he blew on, and then sipped his coffee again and, finally, yawned. It was the greatest display of absolute disregard for authority that I had ever seen.

'*Beseder, beseder,*' he said, and nodded at her as he walked away.

'Unbelievable. Absolutely unbelievable,' Tamar was saying to me. 'He'll show you how to work the machine now.'

I got up and caught a sideway glance in M's direction before following my new mentor into the dishwasher area.

He was sitting down on an upturned basin. His cup of coffee was moving slowly back and forth under the peak of his red cap. It was an army cap with a white emblem of two outstretched wings and an open parachute in the middle. He wore a white T-shirt and green combat trousers, which were pulled down over his red army boots. He fumbled inside the side pocket of his trousers and pulled out a crushed packet of Noblesse cigarettes. Sliding a bent cigarette out from the packet, he straightened it between his two fingers, and then it disappeared under his hat. He stretched out his leg and searched the side pocket for a light. Raising his cap, he saw my feet, and inched his head up slowly towards me.

'*Ma?*' he asked me, the cigarette still in his mouth. He looked a bit like Jim Morrison, the singer from The Doors, but with a heavy tan.

'Can you show me how this thing works?' I asked him.

'Have you got a light?' he asked, and I noticed a slight American accent.

'Yeah, but I think Tamar would freak out if she caught you smoking in here.'

He looked at me, and then standing up, took the cigarette out of his mouth.

'*Tov,*' he said, stretched himself, and then looked at the machine in front of us as if he'd never even noticed it in the room until just then.

The dishwasher itself took up most of the space and was divided into three shining stainless steel sections. The first part was exposed and had chains with square plastic trays lying flat on them. The second part was the cleaning section behind three large sliding doors. The diners would place the dirty dishes and the cutlery on the moving trays, before inching into the next hidden section of noise and boiling water and soap, until eventually, they emerged out of the final section, washed, clean and piping hot. It was here that I had to stand, pick up each piece and place it into its own designated spot.

We both stood and contemplated the silent machine. I was afraid to turn and face Itai in case he had fallen asleep. The section where the dirty dishes were placed was piled high. M and another girl came around the corner with their trays of breakfast dishes.

'Hi,' she called over to me.

I waved.

'What are you doing?' she asked.

I shrugged.

'Okay, bye,' she said and opened the door to leave. Her friend walked out ahead of her, and M turned to look back at me. I couldn't help but watch her as she left, and I noticed a slightly hurt expression. As I turned away, I faced Itai. He was looking at me.

'How long have you been here?' he said.

'Nearly a week,' I said. 'Why?'

'Just wondering.'

'We better get this thing going,' I said.

'Okay,' he said, and he raised his cap, scratched his hair, and then placed the cap back on his head.

'They put the dishes there, you see.'

I nodded.

'The machine washes them in there, okay?'

I nodded again.

'You take the clean cups and plates and knives and everything else, and you put it here behind you, where it's supposed to go. Simple?'

'Simple,' I said.

'I'll be back later,' he said, slapped me on the back and walked out.

I stood on my own looking at the machine for nearly a minute before running out, down the stairs and out into the sun. I saw Itai and ran over to him.

'*Ma?*' he asked me, his lit cigarette in his mouth.

'How do you switch the machine on?'

For the next two hours I stood in my spot while the metallic beast snorted and breathed steam and hot water at me. My hands weren't used to the hot surfaces so I burnt my fingers regularly. Often, I wasn't able to keep up with the speed of the trays, and they'd circle around again for another washing. Itai came back at about ten, and said he'd show me how to wash the machine, as it needed a proper clean once a day in order to avoid cockroaches feeding off the food that washed off the dishes.

Even though it was only ten o'clock, the sweat was already rolling off me. There was no air circulating in the room and the large steam and boiling water-spouting machine beside me wasn't helping matters. Itai stood for a few seconds beside me, and then leaned over to a switch on the wall and flicked it down. A large circular fan about the size of a truck wheel suspended from the ceiling pointed directly at me. When the blades were going full throttle, the resultant air flow was strong enough to move my hair, and I felt instant relief.

'Thanks for showing me that,' I said.

'You're welcome,' he replied, not noticing the lashings of sarcasm in my tone.

The next hour was an intensity of cleaning, scrubbing and washing. Surprisingly, Itai washed twice as hard and twice as fast as me, while at the same time showing me how the machine worked and what to do when minor problems occurred.

'Otherwise, it's Ido's problem,' he kept saying.

At first I thought he was invoking the name of Ido as a sort of deity or Allah figure, in that whenever big problems arose it was the mysteries of Ido at work. It was only later that I found out Ido was an actual mortal and held the position of Maintenance Manager in the kibbutz. Whereas I was imagining myself having to hike to the top of a mountain in order to receive enlightenment on the intricacies of the dishwasher, in fact all I had to do was dial 232 from any kibbutz phone.

When the machine was finally clean, Itai stood and regarded it for almost a full minute, his blues eyes, quite an uncommon eye colour for an Israeli, expertly surveyed and studied every section.

'Okay,' he said finally. 'Coffee?' Later, I saw Tamar sneaking in and examining his work but then leave without comment or complaint.

Beside the water boiler was a small table with glass jars of tea bags, coffee, chocolate powder and sweeteners. The first time I had made a cup of coffee there (I had long since run out of my stash of Irish Lyon's tea bags, and had tried the Israeli generic brand, which failed me miserably, leaving coffee as my only option) I had used a dark powder, bits of which had remained stubbornly on the surface of the coffee. I had tried several times to drink around this thin floating irritation but at each attempt, my teeth, lips and tongue would be left with a film of tiny hard bits that I needed to pick or spit out of my mouth. Of course, I was so engrossed in doing this that I didn't notice that everyone else at the table was watching me and sniggering. Charlie informed me that there are two types of coffee – instant coffee called 'nes' and this other type called 'cafe Turki'. I wanted to know how to drink this other stuff as it smelled much better than the nes, but none of the volunteers seemed to know. Anyway, it was this Turkish coffee that I now saw Itai throwing a large spoonful of into his cup.

'How do you drink it without tasting all the hard bits?' I asked him.

'It falls down to the bottom when you add the sugar,' he explained. 'It just takes a minute.'

'Oh, I see,' I said. 'But doesn't that then leave a pile of coffee at the bottom?'

'Yeah, it's called botz. Botz in English is... how do you call it...? Mud.'

'But,' I said, still not happy with his explanation and thinking of this thick percolating layer of coffee grains at the bottom of the cup. 'What happens when you're finished drinking the coffee and you get to the botz?'

He looked at me as if I were an imbecile. 'You stop drinking and leave the botz,' he said.

We walked down the steps of the rear exit of the dining room and sat under the shade of an olive tree drinking our Turkish coffee. He lit a cigarette from a fresh pack and offered me one. It felt good sitting in the shade, drinking and smoking. Perhaps, I thought, I was getting a little used to the heat. Acclimatising, I suppose. Itai leaned his head back against the trunk of the tree and closed his eyes. He smoked meditatively, his eyes remaining shut, his inhales and exhales long and languid.

'Are you a member of the kibbutz?' I asked him.

With the cup held to his lips, he spat out the coffee with clichéd comedic timing.

'Are you crazy?' he gasped. 'In this place?'

'So why are you here, then?' I asked.

'Because I have to. It's my army duty.'

'Really?' I said, looking around us. A bird was hopping on the branch of the tree we were sitting under, picking at the unripened olives. A child in a yellow dress was hanging upside down in the playground. An old lady in a motorised wheelchair zoomed by, pursued on foot by her flagging Filipino carer.

'It doesn't seem like much of a war zone to me.'

'I have to keep going back to my base every few months.'

'And you're here now to do what? Teach people how the dishwasher works?' I asked.

'No, I am, you know... a parachuter.'

'You're a paratrooper?'

'Yes, paratrooper,' he said and pointed to the white winged emblem on his cap

'So why are you here on the kibbutz and not, I don't know, paratrooping?'

'It's all part of it,' he explained. 'First year, the kibbutz. Second year, training and army. Then I come here for six months, then army for six months.'

'For how long?'

'Four years in total.'

'And the girls are for two years?' I asked.

'If they choose to be in the kibbutz, then three years.'

'Does everyone have to do it?'

'Yeah, unless you're religious,' he said.

'What? If you believe in God then you don't have to go to the army?'

'No,' he laughed. 'It's not that easy. Only if you're an Orthodox Jew.'

'You mean those guys with the black clothes and hats?'

'Yes.'

'That must piss you off, does it?'

'What? That they don't have to go to the army? Not really.'

'And who else doesn't have to go?'

'Israelis that are Arabs.'

'And the girls?'

'If they are pregnant or married or crazy,' he said.

'Crazy?'

'Yeah,' he said. 'You know, mental problems.'

'I see.'

I lay on my back and blew the cigarette smoke into the tree wondering if it would give the olives a smokey taste.

'Are you friends with M?' he asked me.

'No, I wouldn't say friends. Maybe we could have been.'

'What do you mean?'

'I mean, I was chatting all yesterday to her, but I didn't know that she was fifteen years old,' I said sitting up, a little embarrassed.

'And?'

'And?' I repeated. 'She's only fifteen.'

'So? My friend Nathan is twenty-one, and he's been trying to talk to her for the last six months.'

'But she's too young?'

'For who? You?'

'Not just for me,' I said. 'For everyone.'

'No. Next year she will start her initiation into the army. I spent my teenage years in America. Fifteen years old in Israel is not like fifteen years old in the West. They grow up fast here.'

I shook my head, disregarding what he had said. Fifteen was fifteen no matter where you are, but I didn't try to argue with him.

'Where are you from?' he asked me.

'Ireland.'

'Really, what part?'

'Dublin,' I said. 'Why, have you been there?'

'No. I used to go out with a girl from Cork. She was on the kibbutz last year. A volunteer like you.'

'Oh, right. And what happened?'

'Nothing,' he said, turning his attention away from me. 'She went back to Ireland.'

'And you broke her heart?' I joked with him.

'No,' he said.

'Have you spoken to her since she left?'

'No.'

'What was her name,' I asked.

'Marie.'

'Poor Marie,' I laughed. 'She's probably still crying back in Ireland for her exotic Israeli boyfriend.'

He stood up and threw the remains of his coffee and botz onto the ground.

'You're okay on the machine now?' he asked.

'Yeah, thanks,' I said and he nodded, then turned and walked off through the olive trees.

Lunchtime came and went. Charlie popped in every now and then, and we sneaked out for cigarettes. Aengus and Guy came by on their lunch break to gloat at my misfortune. They found little to gloat over however. I had the radio on and felt in good form. My hands had got used to the hot surfaces, and I'd found my rhythm in sorting out the cutlery as it came out of the machine. I knew what I had to do and I got on with doing it, so no one annoyed or bothered me. I was practically my own boss in an obsequious sort of a way.

It was about three o'clock and my working day was coming to an end. The last of the pots and pans from the kitchen had been loaded, and I was working my way through them. A cassette tape, Rod Stewart's Greatest Hits, which I had borrowed from Aengus, played 'The Killing of Georgie', competing for air space with the thunderous noise of the dishwasher.

'Hi,' a voice shouted behind me.

I jumped a little and turned around. She had on a white T-shirt, jeans and an expectant smile across her face. A khaki coloured canvas bag hung over her shoulder. It had handwritten Hebrew text along the strap and a tape cassette of Sting poked out of a side pocket.

'Hi,' I replied, smiling and continuing with my work.

'How is it here?' she asked.

'It's okay,' I said, still working. 'A bit hotter than the kitchens anyway.'

She smiled again but said nothing. There was a silence. A silence of slight embarrassment and awkwardness.

'Okay so, bye,' she said and then turned and left.

I felt silly and quite adolescent. My heart was racing. It was a shock to me how much another's mere presence could affect me. I turned off the machine and leaned my arms against it. Rod Stewart took advantage of the silence and boomed louder.

'Did I do something wrong?' she said.

She stood, feet together, her demure expression tinged with a shred of hurt.

'No,' I said. 'Of course not. It's just that...'

I searched for the words.

'I'm sorry,' I started again. 'It's just that, well... I thought... well, I was hoping that we could, but then... so it's probably best if I don't... or if we...'

She looked at me, trying to comprehend my incoherent babble.

'You're fifteen,' I said. 'I didn't know.'

'So?'

'So, I'm not.'

'Not what?'

'Not fifteen.'

'How old are you?'

'Too old.'

'How old?'

'Twenty.'

'And I'm too young for you, yes?'

'Yes.'

'Why? You like older girls?'

'Yes. No, Christ. It's not that. I just think that fifteen is too...'

'Young?'

'Yes.'

'Okay.'

'But I would love to have... I mean, you're... well, you're absolutely lovely.'

Like a fool I blushed.

'Okay,' she said nodding. Then she turned around and left.

I felt utterly drained. My head was spinning, and I let out a deep sigh.

'And if I were sixteen?'

'Jesus,' I said, jumping again. 'Stop scaring the shit out of me.'

'Well?' she asked.

'Well what?'

'If I were sixteen?'

I laughed.

'You're laughing at me?'

'Christ, no. Em, sixteen, maybe. I don't know.'

She stood there looking at me. It was only then I noticed the necklace she was wearing. Hanging from the simple black rope was a sand-coloured stone pendant, with a naturally formed hole in the centre. It looked golden next to her darkly tanned skin.

'Who is it?' she asked, nodding towards the tape player. Rod Stewart was serenading her for me with 'The First Cut is the Deepest.'

'It's Rod Stewart.'

'Irish?'

'Scottish.'

'Can I listen at home... take it...?'

'Borrow?'

'Yes, borrow,' she smiled.

'Sure.'

I reached up and switched it off and handed her the cassette. Silence descended on the room. I was positive she could hear my heart pounding as I handed it to her. She took the tape without touching my hand and put it in her bag.

'Thank you.'

I nodded, knowing that Aengus would kill me.

'This Saturday...' she began.

'Yeah, sure,' I said. 'You can hang on to it.'

'No. This Saturday,' she started again. 'This Saturday is my birthday.'

I looked at her.

'I will be sixteen then,' she said, and she walked away.

With the music stopped and the machine turned off, silence prevailed. There was a serenity in the room that hadn't been there since the early morning. A light breeze from the open window brushed over me, and I could hear the birds outside chirping contently again.

That evening, I decided it could wait no longer. It was wrong of me to keep Hannah hanging on. Time to 'man up', to 'face the music', and, most definitely, to 'bite the bullet'. I mean, it wasn't like she was going to freak out or something, right? She would understand, surely? It was hardly like we were even actually going out, was it? Yes, I was determined. Determined and decisive. No matter what, I would go and have a chat with her. Tomorrow. Most certainly tomorrow. Tomorrow night.

While Charlie and Aengus had peacefully snored their way through the afternoon and then gone for something to eat, I had happily sauntered my way through *Catch-22*. I thought it best that I didn't go to supper this evening either. It was inevitable therefore, I suppose, that before Charlie and Aengus returned from the dining room, there was a familiar knock on the door. Before waiting for a response though, it pushed open.

'Hallo,' Hannah called out.

I thought about lying perfectly still, like an animal pretending to be dead when threatened by a predator, but I knew she wouldn't be so easily deceived.

'Hi,' I called to her feebly, not sure what Charlie might have said to her this time.

'I hear you're still not feeling too good?'

Thank you, Charlie.

'Yes, but I'll be fine though,' I said.

She came and sat on the side of the bed, and placed her hand on my forehead.

'My poor baby,' she said. 'Are you not hungry?'

'No. I might have some toast later.'

'I should have brought you some food from the dining room.'

'No, really. That would be too much,' I rubbed my stomach for effect. 'Were there many people in the dining room?'

'Just some families and some teenage girls.'

I sat up.

'Really? Which ones?'

'Which ones?'

'Which teenagers?'

'I don't know. About four girls on their own.'

'Which girls?' I asked.

'I don't know.'

'What did they look like?'

'What?'

'The girls,' I said. 'Describe them.'

'Describe them?'

'Yeah, did they have brown hair? Was it long?'

'Are you crazy?'

'What?'

'Why do you want to know about the teenage girls?'

I lay back down.

'No reason,' I said. 'Em... one of them owes me a cassette.'

'I think you are a little delirious.'

'No, I'll be fine. It's just my stomach.'

She reached under the blanket and rubbed my stomach with her hand.

'Is that any better?' she asked.

'Thank you,' I said, laid back and closed my eyes. Perhaps if I pretended to sleep under her hypnotic massage she might just leave.

She rubbed gently in circular motions. 'That's much better,' I said.

She slid her hand from right to left gently caressing my sides.

'That's nice,' I said and sunk my head further into the pillow.

Suddenly, her hand dropped down, and she started to caress my crotch. It caught me completely off guard, and I got such a shock that I bolted upright in the bed. This obviously wasn't what she was expecting, as her head was moving downwards at the same time. Our heads clashed together with such a bang that I fell back down onto the bed just as she collapsed backwards onto the floor.

'Fuck,' I cried holding my head with my hand.

I looked at her sideways on the floor.

'*Scheisse*,' she groaned, her right hand nursing her right eye.

'Are you okay?' I asked her.

The door opened, and the main light was turned on.

'What the fuck?' Aengus said, Charlie standing behind him. Hannah got up off the floor, obviously embarrassed, and stumbled her way towards the door, her hand still pressed against her eye.

'Hannah,' I called to her.

'We'll talk later,' she mumbled and left.

'If you don't want to go out with her, just tell her,' Charlie said, once Hannah had closed the door. 'There's no need to resort to violence.'

'Now that's what I call fighting them off,' Aengus said.

'I think I've my cracked my head,' I said.

Charlie walked over to me and looked at my forehead. I lifted my hand to show him where we'd collided.

'Nasty,' he said. 'That's going to leave a mark.'

'A Deutsche Mark,' Aengus added.

'Cheers,' I said.

'Would you like some good news then?' Aengus asked me.

'Go on,' I said.

'You're in the hatzer tomorrow,' he said.

'The what?'

'The hatzer,' he said. 'I think it means yard or something like that.'

'It's driving around with Itai all day, avoiding work,' Charlie said. 'That's what it is.'

'Itai?' I asked.

'Yeah,' Charlie said, opening a beer. 'Itai who showed you the dishwasher today. It's probably to help him because of the wedding on Saturday.'

'What wedding?' I asked.

'Jesus,' Aengus grumbled. 'You'll never find out anything unless you get out of this fucking room.'

I ate the food that the lads had brought me, had a couple of beers and even slipped outside for a quick cigarette, getting Charlie to check first that Hannah wasn't around.

'You'll be lucky if she's not unconscious in her room after the whack you gave her, mate,' Charlie said.

I could feel with my fingertips the protrusion of a definite bump on my forehead. No one lit a fire outside, and everyone seemed to be in bed by eleven.

'Charlie,' I called out later when Aengus was asleep.

I lay on my bed staring up at the ceiling, my open book resting on my chest. I could hear him breathing deeply.

'Charlie,' I said a little louder.

'What?' he said drowsily.

'Was M there tonight?' I asked.

'What?'

'Did you see M in the dining room tonight?

'Jesus,' he said. 'You've got to let that go, mate.'

'I know,' I said. He turned over onto his side.

'But was she there?' I asked. There was no reply for a few seconds and I thought he'd drifted off to sleep.

'Yes, she was there,' he finally said.

'And did she look like she was...? I don't know...'

'What? Looking for you?'

'Yeah,' I said, a little embarrassed.

The small fan whizzed from side to side.

'I suppose so,' he said.

I breathed a deep sigh and smiled into the darkness.

'Thanks,' I said, but there was no reply.

10

I think it's important to have moments in our lives when we take stock of not only who but where we are at that precise time. To look at what we're doing from an omniscient point of view and to question ourselves from a contemplative and meditative perspective and with the ultimate soul-searching question: How the fuck exactly did I end up where I am right now? And it doesn't always have to be a question of a malignant nature or tone, or even need wait for a situation of misfortune to arise. It can be asked just as easily, and even more importantly, with appreciation and self-reflecting joy. In fact, if you don't find cause to ask yourself that question every now and again, then you're missing out. Missing out on what? Well, I suppose that's something only you can find out.

I found myself asking that very question the next morning. I was speeding along, standing on the back of a trailer. The trailer itself was full of junk and rubbish, and was being pulled by Itai, who was bobbing up and down on a tractor seat in front of me. The current of air against my face was warm as I clung on to the shovels and brushes that were strapped to the sides. The ground was hard and bumpy, and the trailer had a prehistoric suspension system, but I felt fantastic.

Earlier that morning, after a breakfast of coffee and cigarettes, we had walked the short distance from the dining room to where the tractor was parked, and I had climbed onto the open trailer bed. Itai had mounted the tractor, as if straddling a horse, and when he had started the engine, the trailer had begun rattling even before the tractor had moved an inch. Then he had driven up and down the roads of the kibbutz, stopping at every bin and skip.

He didn't seem to be a morning person, so we mostly worked in silence. When the trailer was packed with sawn-off branches and bushes, and other bits of wood, we drove through the back gates of the kibbutz and went full-tilt through the desert – not that full-tilt was all that tilting.

After about five minutes, we came to a large trench that had been excavated. It was a pit big enough to take several cars. Half of it was already filled with shrubbery and dried out trees. Itai stopped the tractor and reversed the trailer so that the back door was sitting over the hole. I jumped off, Itai pulled down a lever, and the tractor's engine revved loudly. He walked to the back and opened the door. Eventually, and with great effort, like an old man trying to take a piss, the hydraulic fluid pumped reluctantly into the extendable struts of the trailer. One end of the trailer ascended into the air and out slid its entire cargo. Once it was empty again, we drove back into the kibbutz, the tractor gaining speed when the road surface changed from sand to tarmac.

The roads throughout the kibbutz were tarmacked, and most were shaded by tall palm, pine or eucalyptus trees. Small groups of olive trees were also scattered around, and little gardens of delicate-looking cactus plants seemed to be planted here and there, as if at a garden lover's whim. We turned right, driving past the wood shop, the metal shop and then down a smaller road that eventually led us to the back of the garage. Itai stopped the tractor alongside a diesel pump and cut the engine.

'Do you want me to fill it up?' I asked him.

'No, we'll do it in a minute,' he said climbing down. 'Let's have a quick coffee first.'

Several cars with their bonnets open, or simply missing, lay half- assembled or disassembled in the darkened corrugated building, like battle-injured soldiers in a field hospital. Broken parts lay on the ground in pools of oil; stained spanners and blackened tools rested on the engines. I followed Itai to a small hidden alcove, not dissimilar to a snug in a pub; there three men sat drinking coffee under a cloud of cigarette smoke.

Itai shook hands with the youngest of them, a blond guy, in a brotherly way. The eldest man started to give out to Itai as he made the coffee, but he wasn't shouting at him, it was more like talking extremely loud so that there was no possibility of anyone interrupting him. Itai responded but in his usual hushed and nonchalant tone; the agitated man laughed at whatever it was Itai had said. The last member of the crew, a beer-bellied balding man in his late forties, waved his hands and asked Itai something. He reminded me of a slightly younger version of the actor Buster Merryfield who played Uncle Albert in the BBC television series *Only Fools and Horses*. He spoke in Hebrew, of course, but his accent was unlike anything I'd heard before. Itai barely replied to the man, before turning around and asking me, 'you want coffee?'

All eyes turned to me.

I nodded.

All eyes turned away.

The eldest man started 'shouting' again, as Itai handed me my coffee and then sat down beside the blonde guy, punching him hard on his thigh. The blonde guy bent forward in exaggerated pain.

'Here, son. Sit down here,' Uncle Albert said.

I sat down beside him, not at all surprised that he not only looked but also spoke like Uncle Albert.

'Where's you from, then?' he asked me, his cockney accent even stronger than Charlie's.

'Ireland,' I said.

'Oh oooo,' he said, as if someone had surprised him with a birthday cake, or perhaps a freshly opened can of Heineken. 'Here, Levi, we've got another Irishman here.'

Levi, the eldest man, barely offered him a sideways glance in reply and continued his conversation with Itai.

'We had another couple of Irishmen here for the summer,' Uncle Albert said. 'A right pair they was. Jimmy and Chris. Did we have some sessions together? Now that would be telling, wouldn't it? That would be telling. Oh ooooh.'

'Where were they from?' I asked.

'Couple of Dublin lads they was,' he said. 'A right pair, all right.'

What is it about fellow countrymen and women that, although they are strangers to us when we are at home, we feel this need to become their friends when we are abroad? I could happily walk by several hundred people in O'Connell Street without barely offering them a sideways glance, and yet if any one of them were here on the kibbutz in Israel, or in a hostel in Thailand or even in an Irish pub in Sydney, I'd just as happily go out of my way to introduce myself to them, as I'm sure they would introduce themselves to me.

'Really?' I said. 'And where did they work?'

'Jimmy worked in the chicken houses, I think. And Chris had Itai's job.'

'What?' I asked. 'A volunteer had Itai's job?'

'Yeah, he did it for a couple of months during the summer.'

'But how... I mean, did he...'

'Did he what?'

'Did he drive the tractors?' I asked.

'Course.'

'How did he manage with the language? Could he speak Hebrew?'

'What Chris? Hebrew? You must be joking,' Uncle Albert said. 'Most people speak English here.'

I cast Itai a mutinous look as he sipped his coffee. I heard the rear door of the garage open and then slam shut. A man came in and started shouting at Itai. Itai waved him off with several flicks of the back of his hand but stood up anyway. He nodded at me that we should go.

'What's your name?' I asked. 'I can't keep calling you Uncle Albert.'

'What?' Uncle Albert said.

'I'm Joseph,' I said.

'Arthur,' he replied, and he held out his hand. 'Nice to meet you, Joe.' Oh, right. I forgot. So, Aengus and Arthur were the only two that called me 'Joe'.

'You going down the pub tonight?' I asked him.

'Does the pope shit in the woods, Joe?' he asked, and I forced a smile.

The intruder was walking back outside and still shouting at Itai. Itai still looked unimpressed. Another tractor, but a smaller one, was parked behind Itai's tractor, waiting to fill up with fuel. Itai removed the flexible arm of the diesel pump and opened the round cap on the top of the fuel tank. Obviously, this guy wasn't at all impressed that Itai hadn't even bothered to fill up before going inside, and he launched into a new tirade of vernacular abuse.

When we drove back and parked behind the dining room, I found out the real reason I was working with Itai that day. There was indeed going to be a wedding on the kibbutz the next day, Saturday, and Itai was responsible for bringing most of the tables and chairs from where they were stored in a bomb shelter at the back of the dining room to the main grass area. For the next two hours we carried, toiled, banged knuckles, trapped fingers, stubbed toes and sweated and sweated until the grass was covered with enough tables and chairs for about four hundred people. Other teams were responsible for setting up banners, exterior lights and a stage to host the newlyweds. People buzzed by on their bicycles carrying bags, boxes and even their children, who were strapped into front and rear carrier chairs. A woman with short dark hair cycled right in front of me, and I saw her purse fall and land silently on the grass. I dropped the table that I was carrying with Itai, and ignoring his shouts, picked up the purse and raced after her.

'*Merci*,' she said when I handed her back her purse.

'You're welcome,' I replied, and she smiled.

It was twelve o'clock by the time we'd finished, and I felt so worn out that I decided not to bother going in for lunch, but instead I bought a Coke from the Colbo and lay in the shade of a tree for a while. I closed my eyes and listened to the sounds of the birds above me, children playing nearby and bicycles freewheeling down the paths. I felt myself falling asleep, my breath growing deeper, my fingers loosening their grip around the Coke bottle.

'You work hard, I see,' she said.

I opened my eyes, blinking from the brightness and saw M standing above me.

'Hi,' I mumbled.

'You were sleeping?' she asked.

'No, no. Just resting my eyes,' I said.

'Well, you looked asleep.'

'No, just enjoying a well-deserved rest.'

'Desert rest?'

'No, not desert rest, although technically I suppose it is,' I said. 'Deserved rest. It means I earned it. I worked for it.'

'What work?'

I pointed towards all the tables and chairs.

'*Ah. Ha chtuna*,' she said.

I looked questioningly at her. 'The weeding tomorrow,' she said.

'Wedding,' I corrected her.

'The wedding,' she repeated.

'Who are the victims?' I asked.

'The...?'

'Who's getting married?'

'Ilan and Ilana,' she said.

'Ilan and Ilana? Sounds more like a pop duo.'

She looked me up and down in silence, her hesitant eyes considering me as if studying an abstract painting.

'What?' I asked.

'What?' she repeated, her eyes returning to look at me.

'What are you thinking about?'

'I'm going for a walk later up to the hill,' she said quickly, as if she'd rehearsed saying it several times. 'Would you like to come with me?'

I stared up at her and she blushed, and then she turned her gaze away. I sat up.

'A walk?' I asked her.

'Yes,' she said turning back to me. 'To the hill.' She pointed towards something in the distance, and I looked, not quite sure what I was looking at. There were some hills in view on the horizon, just above the top of the trees. I turned my attention back to her and now it was my turn to study her in silence. She looked over her shoulder towards the colbo a little impatiently and then back to me.

'Well?' she said.

'I'm not so sure if...'

'I spoke to my *imma*, and she said it's okay,' she blurted out. Again rehearsed.

'Your *imma*?' I asked, picturing some sort of spiritual guru.

'My *imma*, yes. My mother.'

'What?' I said standing up quickly. 'You asked your mother... you asked your mother what exactly?'

I was talking too loudly, and she took a step back.

'If I could go for a walk with a volunteer,' she said.

'And she said yes?'

'Yes.'

'But she doesn't even know me.'

'She told me that she met you today.'

'Today?'

'Yes.'

'I never met your mother today,' I said. 'I don't even know who...' Suddenly, I remembered the woman on the bike.

'Ah, I see,' I said.

'She told me that you seem a nice boy and that it is okay to go for walk but not in the dark.'

I looked at her and without realising it, I was nodding.

'Okay?' she asked.

'Yes,' I said. 'Okay. When?'

'Five o'clock.'

'We meet here?' I asked.

'No,' she said quickly, looking over her shoulder again. 'You know the road beside the tea house?'

'The tea house? Oh, you mean the pub?'

'Yes, there. You know?'

'Sure,' I said and she smiled. 'See you there, so.'

'Bye,' she said, turned around and walked away. I watched her leave for a moment and then bent down and picked up my

Coke. I looked at the dining room and saw Itai sitting on a bench smoking a cigarette.

We spent another two hours working; thirty minutes of which we drove around the kibbutz, then another thirty minutes back in the garage drinking coffee and finally a full hour listening to him bash the hell out of a set of drums that he stored in an uninhabited caravan near the perimeter fence.

By four o'clock I was sitting on my bed, showered, changed and ready for my walk or my date or whatever it was. I gnawed on the nails of my right hand, looked at my watch and then lay down on the bed again in an attempt to read. After a few sentences, I sat up again, looked at my watch and then gnawed on the nails of my left hand. Charlie and Aengus were outside with a lot of the other volunteers enjoying the late afternoon warmth and drinking beers. I hadn't told them my plans for that afternoon and feared that some of them were starting to think me a little strange because of my constant lack of 'joining in'.

I paced the room. I wanted to go and wait near the pub, but I could hear Hannah's voice outside, and I still didn't feel just quite ready for any confrontation with her. I sat on the bed again and noticed with annoyance that my right knee was hopping up and down – a nervous twitch. I slapped my hand down on it, only to find that as soon as it stopped, the left knee took up the beat. I read, paced, gnawed and inspected my watch until finally I heard Hannah saying goodbye to the others.

Checking my appearance one more time in the mirror, I pushed down the handle of the door and opened it slowly. Sticking my head out first, I saw eight heads turn in silence to watch the creaking door.

'Hi,' I said.

No one replied.

'Just going for a bit of a walk,' I told them all, as casual sounding as I could make it.

'Have a good one,' Californian Chad said.

'Thanks,' I replied and walked down the path, almost tiptoeing away.

'By the way,' Charlie called out. I froze like an escaping prisoner caught in a searchlight.

'Yeah?' I asked, turning only my head back to him.

'Don't forget it's Shabbat meal tonight, and it starts at seven sharp,' he said. I turned around to face him. He looked me in the eye and winked at me.

'Thanks,' I said, smiled back at him and walked away.

The two white wooden buildings that made up the pub and the disco stood silently in their mellow green surroundings. I was early, but happy to be out of the room. I sat on one of the benches in the little courtyard that separated the two buildings and smoked contentedly.

I had been on the kibbutz for almost a week now and, as I had done a hundred times already that week, I thought about home. I thought about what I would be doing at that particular time if I were back in Dublin. I'd have just finished work and would be thinking and talking with friends about the weekend. But, despite all well-meaning discussions, we would always end up drinking in one of three possible locations. The autumn days would be inching ever colder and ever darker, like a shadow sliding slowly down the wall of a well. Reluctant children and their equally reluctant teachers already returned to school. The traffic would be getting busier and noisier under darker skies. Heavier coats worn over thicker tops. More sensible shoes walking on wetter streets.

It wasn't until she was only a few feet away that I noticed M walking towards me, her footsteps waking me from my reverie. 'Shalom,' she said.

'Shalom,' I replied.

Encouraged by my Hebrew effort, she followed with 'Ma'ha'in'yaim?'

'I'm afraid I'm going to have to stop you there,' I said smiling.

'How are you? Ma-ah-neh-nim?'

I attempted to say it several times, but my mouth felt like it was practising some new yoga moves.

'How do you answer by saying "all right"?' I asked.

'*Beseder.*'

'Ah, now that's not too bad. Beh-se-der.'

'Exactly,' she said. '*Beseder.*'

'So, if I were to say "*beseder*" and raise my tone at the end, like in French, wouldn't that be okay to ask someone "*beseder?*" instead of that other complicated thing?'

'Yes, it would even be *beseder*,' she answered smiling. 'But it would also be very, very lazy.'

I smiled and stubbed out my cigarette in the ashtray.

'How long is this walk going to be for?' I said, nodding at the small blue haversack that was hanging from her shoulder. 'We're not spending the night up there, are we?'

She laughed, a little embarrassed and self-conscious. 'Of course not. Just some water and snacks.'

'Snacks?' I asked. 'What snacks?'

'You'll see.' She looked over her shoulder as if making sure that no one was there.

'We go?' she asked.

'We go,' I answered. 'Unless you'd rather just wait here for the pub to open?'

'I'm not allowed in the pub.'

'Why not?' I asked.

'I must to be eighteen first,' she said and walked off.

She had only walked a few feet before she realised that I wasn't following. She turned back around to face me. The reminder of her age was like a soft slap in the face.

'What?' she asked.

'It's just... em...,' I mumbled.

'Just what?'

'I keep forgetting... your age.'

She stared at me with a look that I was unable to read.

'You're fifteen,' I reminded her and myself also.

'I'll be sixteen tomorrow,' she informed me, with a slight smack of anger in her tone.

'Yes, but still...' I said.

'I am going for walk,' she said and shoved the haversack further up her arm. 'If you want to come, you come. If you want to go home, so go home.'

'No wait,' I said and jumped down from the table and caught up with her. 'Are you sure?'

'Yes. I am sure. I even asked my mother's permission and she said it is okay,' she smiled at me.

'Maybe I'm the one that should be asking my mother's permission?'

'Perhaps you should also warn her that I am a Jewish girl?'

'Christ,' I said. 'You're Jewish as well? When were you going to tell me?'

She laughed and hit me on the arm

'Okay, let's go then,' I said.

'*Beseder?*'

'*Beseder,*' I repeated.

We walked the short distance from the pub to the perimeter fence without speaking but without any awkwardness in the silence either. At the gates, she turned and walked along the fence. In less than a minute, we stopped at a section where the fence was loose at the bottom and could be lifted up, allowing us to easily crawl under it. She lifted the fence, and I crept under. On the other side, I did the same for her and then we patted the dust off our hands and knees.

'You've done that before, haven't you?' I asked.

She nodded, smiling at me.

'And what were all the other boys' names?' As I said it, I realised half way through, that it was a stupid thing to say, but it was too late.

'No,' she protested. 'I never... I usually am on my own...'

'I'm sorry. I didn't mean it that way. I know. Sorry.'

I made a big deal about patting all the sand and dust off myself loudly.

'Is it this way?' I asked, randomly pointing somewhere, desperate to change the subject.

'No,' she said pointing. 'It's there.'

There was a series of smooth hills on the opposite side of the main road that ran past the kibbutz. I could hear the distant drone of cars punching the air with noise as they whizzed by. A thin line of trees separated the road from the base of the hills. The hills themselves looked like huge bald men sticking their heads up out of the sandy ground; they were patchy with clumps of drying and dying green and brown bushes. On the other side of the road, I saw a small orchard that seemed overgrown and dotted with randomly planted trees of various species. It stood out from its grubby and dry surroundings like a streak of sunlight on a cloudy day.

'What's that?' I asked M.

'It's called *paradis*,' she said.

'Paradise? Perhaps we can go in there someday?'

'Yes. I always go there with the boys I bring for a walk.'

'I'm sure you do,' I smiled.

I told her about the night I'd seen the teenagers slicing up the chickens. She said she'd only seen it once and almost got sick.

'Was that the teenagers' clubhouse?' I asked her.

'No, that's where they live.'

'They all live there?'

'Sure,' she said. 'When a child on the kibbutz becomes a teenager, they move to the teenagers' housing and share a room with someone.'

'So they basically leave home when they are thirteen?'

'Yes. One or two stay at home but not that many.'

'That's very young but I think I like that,' I said.

'Before, it was when they were a baby, and then they go to a baby house.'

'And the parents don't look after the baby?'

'No. They visit only in the evening but the... responsabilité?'

'Responsibility.'

'Of course. The responsibility to raise the child is for the kibbutz,' she explained. 'For the kibbutz, the children are the most important thing.'

We began to climb the largest of the hills, and although it wasn't that steep, there was still some heat left in the sun, and I felt my face growing redder from the effort. I paused after ten minutes and looked back towards the kibbutz.

'Nice view,' I called up to M, who was charging up ahead of me.

'Come on,' she called back. 'Wait till we get to the top.'

As I stopped, I instinctively took out a cigarette from my pocket, looked up at M, who was now a few minutes ahead of me and then slid the cigarette back into the box. 'I hope you have some cold beer in that bag,' I said and followed after her.

I found myself mumbling the words of the David Bowie song again, as I had done though the streets of Tel Aviv, rhythmically raising one knee after the other. Before I knew it, I had caught up with M, who was now sitting on a blanket, her knees folded up to her chest as she watched me climb the last few steps. I collapsed down on the blanket, sitting a little behind her hoping to hide my red face. With my body now still, I could feel my over-worked heart pumping madly, and I tried to control my breathing, so as not to sound like a panting dog.

I looked down the hill we had climbed and at the road where the cars, small and barely audible now, like a little boy's toys, drove by. Raising my head slowly to take in the view, I saw the kibbutz – a green patch of tall trees and mostly single-storey buildings. The swimming pool glistened a light blue; the volunteers' houses looked like square cardboard boxes stacked side by side; the imposing two-storey dining room at the kibbutz's heart. Past the kibbutz stretched miles and miles of flat sandy terrain. Further away on the horizon I could see the peaks of mountains, like dead and dried-out rose thorns, that cut into the skyline causing the heavens to bleed a crimson sky. The sun inched slowly down behind them, like a deep sigh, inky shadows spreading out over the flat ground, as if a dark curtain was closing on the day. The entire landscape's colour and depth changed continually like a large, slow breathing animal.

M said nothing, allowing me the silence to appreciate and even marvel.

'Are you impressed?' she asked me.

The setting sun sat in the sky like an over-ripened orange. It shone its red glow down onto the mountains, the sand, the rocks, on towards the kibbutz, then over the road, up onto the hill before finally settling on M's face. There the light rested, causing her olive skin to radiate from its luminous touch, her exposed neck and shoulders to shine like mahogany, and her dark brown eyes to turn a deep shade of almost amber.

'Yes,' I said. 'I'm very impressed.'

She leaned forwards and picked up the haversack at her feet, opened it and took out two bottles of water, handing one of them to me. I drank the water as she took out a green plastic bag with a photograph of a sunflower on the front.

'What's that?' I asked.

'*Garinim*,' she said and spilled some brown seeds into her hand. 'You like?'

I took a few, examined them between my fingertips and then popped them into my mouth. I crunched the dry, salty seeds. They shattered into shrapnel pieces that pierced my gums and felt impossible to swallow. I spat them out unceremoniously onto the ground beside me, and continued having to spit three or four times until, finally, all trace was gone. Cleaning my teeth with my tongue I turned to M who was looking at me with a look of dismay at best, disgust at worse.

'Got anything else?' I asked, taking a gulp from the water bottle.

'You don't eat like that,' she explained, taking a single seed between her two fingers. 'Like this, you see?'

She took one of the seeds and placed it between her upper and lower front teeth. I slid closer to her to see. Biting down gently on the shell, it opened and cracked into two. Then with the tip of her tongue, she scooped out the tiny seed inside while still holding the empty shell in her hand. She held out the seed, barely visible in her fingertips. Gently, I took it and ate it. I recognised them as the same type of seeds I had seen the woman at the bus station eating a week before.

'Well?' she asked.

'Hardly seems worth all the effort,' I said. 'Got any popcorn?'

She bumped her body off mine and smiled.

I took another one, bit it and managed to prevent most of the seed casing from going into my mouth but was unable to avoid spitting out the last piece.

She laughed and poured a small mound of the seeds into my hand. In front of us, a lucid serenity that seemed frozen in time had settled over the landscape. We sat like visitors in an art gallery, as if carefully studying a large painting with 'Desert at Sunset' as its title.

'It is green where you live?' she asked.

'Yes,' I said. 'Mostly dark green.'

'You are lucky.'

'Oh, yeah. I know. We Irish can't believe our luck. Lucky, lucky, lucky.'

'I love the clouds,' she said. 'Different shapes and sizes.'

'We usually have just one giant cloud sitting over us for most of the year.'

'But you have sun also?'

'Sometimes,' I said. 'And sometimes we can have a warm sun in the morning, rain in the afternoon, cloud in the evening and then a freezing night. Four seasons in one day.'

'Wow. That's amazing.'

'It's amazing all right,' I agreed, trying not to sound too sarcastic.

I suddenly realised that I had hiked up the side of a hill to marvel at this magnificent view, and the best I could do to charm this girl was to talk about the Irish weather.

'You're quite lucky yourself,' I told her. 'It seems like a nice life on a kibbutz.'

'Yes, it is,' she agreed. 'For children and old people.'

'You don't like living here?'

'It's okay,' she said. 'I have my family and my friends, but I want to travel. See all of Europe. Maybe go back to France.'

'So you'll be finished school soon, no?'

'Yes, but after school I have army. For two years.'

'Oh, right,' I said. 'I forgot.'

'You don't have to go to army?'

'Me? No. We have a very small army.'

'A small army is good.'

'You don't want to go to the army?' I asked.

'It does not matter if I want to or don't want to. I must to go.'

'But if you had a choice?'

She thought for a moment, as if she'd never thought about the possibility before. 'If I could to choose,' she said. 'Then no. I don't go to army.'

She shrugged, took another sunflower seed from her palm and bit down on it. She bit without regret or remorse and without any hint of being a victim.

We sat in silence for a while, our bodies slightly touching each other subconsciously. The mound of discarded empty sunflower shells on the blanket at our feet grew steadily taller as we crunched down on the salty seeds, and as I became more proficient at scooping out their minuscule internal treasures. We studied the world below us as if it were our own creation. She looked over her shoulder and up at the sky. In contrast to the red, blue and gold before us, the sky had darkened and was rising steadily behind us like a tidal wave. It had patience to its looming presence though, as if it were waiting for us to leave.

'Shall we go?' I asked.

'Yes,' she said but didn't move. 'Soon.'

We both watched the sun slowly concede its reign over the day and bear witness to a new era approaching; an inevitable changing of the guard; or the start of a new chapter in a book.

Our bodies leaned into one another now, our heads almost touching. 'Thank you for bringing me here,' I said. '*Toda.*'

'*Toda sh'bata,*' she replied. 'Thank you for coming.'

I placed my open hand over her knee for her to take. Instead, misunderstanding my intent, she poured a fresh pile of sunflower seeds into my palm.

The peacefulness of the dusk was broken only by our crunching of shells as they opened in our mouths and offered us up their hearts, which we happily devoured together.

It was dark by the time we crawled back under the perimeter fence. As I patted the dust off my knees, the back of M's shirt got snagged on a loose wire.

'Hold on,' I said, and bent down to untangle her. Freeing her shirt, I took her hand and helped her up. We walked back along the side of the fence and out onto the road near the pub. I remembered Charlie's warning about not being late, and it was only when I checked my watch that I realised I was still holding M's hand.

'I should go this way,' she said when we arrived at the junction in the road. 'It's quick way, and it is late for the meal.'

'Okay,' I said, and took a step away from her while still holding her hand. With our arms outstretched, but still touching, we both smiled, and then let go.

I watched her walk for a moment before turning around. There was most likely a self-satisfied grin on my face when Hannah and Shir emerged from a side street right in front of me. Hannah looked at my face, then turned and saw M walking away, turned back to appraise the now guilt-ridden and sheepish expression I was wearing. Quickly adding two and two together, and coming up with a large six-digit number (which wouldn't be too far from the truth), she attempted to say something, but the sharp words became wedged in her throat. Instead, she just stared open-mouthed at me. I stared at her, and she stared at me. Eventually, Shir took her gently by the elbow and led her away as if she were a witness to a major road accident and would require the obligatory sit-down, being wrapped in a woolly blanket and sipping on an over-sweetened hot cup of tea.

I looked at my watch. Ten minutes to seven. 'Shit,' I said and began to run the remaining distance to my room.

The door opened as I was about to grab the handle. Charlie and Aengus, looking fresh and relaxed, stood in the open doorway. Both were dressed in their 'Sunday best', or 'Shabbat best', I suppose. Panting deeply to catch my breath, my face sunburnt and sweating profusely, I barged past them. I pulled off my white T-shirt, dust and sand falling to the floor, sprayed deodorant under my arms, put on an unironed shirt that I prised from my duffle bag, and then stood impatiently behind Charlie and Aengus, who'd both been observing this performance.

'Are we going, then?' I asked. They shared a disapproving look with one another, like a parent's hopelessness for a disappointing child, and they walked out ahead of me.

We arrived at the dining room just minutes before the Shabbat ceremonies started. Every table was fully seated, and everyone was smartly dressed in either white or bright summer colours. The tables were laid with white tablecloths, place settings, flowers and tall white candles. A notice-board displayed a table map with the various family names scribbled in pencil. Charlie quickly spotted the only word in English 'Volunteers', and we made our way to that table. I glanced furtively around the room and soon caught sight of her. She was dressed in white and was seated with her family of two brothers, her mother and a rather austere and distinguished looking bearded man, whom I assumed to be her father. She spotted me and rewarded my searching eyes with a smile.

I sat beside Charlie and then looked up at the acerbic face in front of me. 'Hi Hannah,' I mumbled, but she turned away.

A guitar was strummed, and the room quietened. The guitar player began singing, and the diners joined him in a reverent chorus of 'Hallelujah.' People swayed unconsciously as they sang, their rocking motion causing the flames from the candles to dance from side to side with them. Parents smiled at their children, some held hands, and one or two leaned across to hush a talkative rebel. Outside the room, darkness had descended. The pathways and homes were quiet and empty. The singing inside seemed a declaration in unison of alliance and friendship; the kibbutz's core of warmth and harmony. Finally, after almost a week, I was starting to see the appeal of living on the kibbutz. It had a definite charm, a charm that had yet to really tempt me at all, but I could see glimpses of why others might find it appealing.

Unlike every other night, on a Friday evening, members of the kibbutz served us our dinner – volunteers never served on a Sabbath. I was given a chicken noodle soup, which I ate with lots of bread. There was also a bottle of cheap Israeli wine placed on every table. Our bottle had been emptied long before I sat down, but, having smelled the aroma from someone else's cup, I didn't feel I had missed out. The main course was chicken, peas and rice. There were bowls of salad served with a vinaigrette dressing, which was tasty, and I poured most of our table's allocation onto my rice and chicken. I was about to shove a forkful of food into my mouth when Hannah stood up.

'Your stomach is better now?' she spat at me and walked out. It was only then that I leaned back into my chair and breathed easily. Charlie gave me an all-knowing and all-seeing smile. I leaned over to his ear.

'I think she's going to kill me tonight,' I whispered.

He considered this. 'Probably,' he replied without smiling.

I turned and saw M walking into the dishwasher area with her plate, accompanied by two other girls. As she walked out, she held the door for her two friends to pass by and then turned her head ever so slightly in my direction.

'So what happens now?' I asked Charlie.

'Well, she'll probably ignore you for a while. She is German, so you have to expect some sort of retaliation.'

'No,' I said. 'I mean what happens now after dinner? The pub isn't open is it?'

'Oh, sorry. I thought you meant... never mind. There's usually some coffee and cake on the lawn, and people sit around for a chat. The pub doesn't open till eleven.'

I hadn't had a cigarette since that afternoon outside the pub, and I suddenly craved some nicotine and caffeine. 'Okay, see you outside,' I said, and stood up with my empty plate and cutlery.

Just as I knew M was aware of my eyes watching her as she left, so too I now felt Charlie's eyes watching me. What must he think of me? I thought to myself.

From the top of the stairs, I tried to spot M but there was quite a crowd now spilling out onto the lawns. There were several tables covered with white tablecloths; people were queuing for coffee and cake, and then finding a chair I imagined beside someone to have a gossip with. The tables and chairs that Itai and I had assembled remained uncovered; the stage and the trees had unlit decorations hanging on them. Six giant wooden Hebrew letters were placed at the edge of the lawn, but of course, I had no idea what they said or whether they were even upside down or back to front.

I poured a coffee and lit a cigarette. Aengus's laughter caught my attention and I walked in the direction I thought it was coming from, but seeing the back of Hannah's head in front of him, I decided to try a different spot. Further away from the dining room and from its light, the grass turned from green to black, and I found myself drawn to its obscurity. The grass was a little cold to touch, and a slight dew had already settled on the ground. I sat on the lawn and watched the kibbutz members and non-members, volunteers and soldiers, children, teenagers and retirees, all mingling and chatting contentedly. I thought of my own family, my parents, brothers and sisters. For the first time, I wished that they could see what I was now observing rather than wishing I could be where they were. Perhaps I could hang on till Christmas before going home. See out my stay in the desert as planned. Then make my way to Australia in the New Year, as I had dreamed of doing.

With only the glow from the tip of my cigarette betraying my secret location, I followed the smoke up into the air and into the innumerable stars. As many stars in the galaxy as I had options in my life.

I can't remember who exactly I was talking to but I do remember hearing someone saying that it was after midnight. I most likely had half a litre of Goldstar sitting in front of me, but I couldn't tell you now whether my glass was completely full or almost empty. From the disco I could hear a song blasting out – the Rolling Stones, I think. Actually, no, I think it was the Beatles, but again I can't be certain. Anyway, it was the person who was sitting opposite me, Guy I think, who saw it happening before I did. Yes, that makes sense because I must have had my back to her. Guy's face, yes, I remember now it was definitely Guy. Guy's face scrunching up as if witnessing a car crash unfolding before him, powerless to stop it. I had barely turned my head to the side when the full pitcher... with that quantity it had to have been a pitcher not a glass... when the full pitcher of Goldstar poured... no not poured, poured would suppose a certain flow whereas this was more of a flop like a wave tumbling and crashing... when a full pitcher of beer crashed down onto my head, bounced off and ricocheted in every direction. Inevitably, a sizeable quantity of the beer remained in my vicinity, but nonetheless I still heard a few disgruntled cries from innocent victims who had been caught in the friendly fire. The wet, cold shock caused me to jump up from the table. There was no denying it: I was soaked. From those people who had not been splashed with beer, I heard muffled giggles.

The top of my jeans was wetter than my shirt. My wet hair had morphed into a fringe that was now blocking my eyes. I stood to one side of the table and wiped my face clean using my hand. A full pitcher of beer emptied over your head is undeniably embarrassing, but compared with what else I might have suffered at the hands of a woman scorned, I thought that I had got off lightly. With that thought in mind, I began to smirk. I suppose it was at the point when I was wiping my wet hair, my smirk broadening into a smile, that I noticed a sudden movement to my left. The fist hit my jaw with such force that it had the effect of spinning me around to face the table. I almost fell onto the table, but Guy stood up quickly and grabbed me by the shoulders. I turned my head just in time to see Hannah marching off defiantly, with Jenny hurrying after her.

11

I was awakened the following morning by the sound of muffled voices outside the door. The room was a mess of piles of clothes, books, used cups and plates and empty beer bottles, flanked on either side by two unmade beds. From where I lay, I could just about make out a line of ants continuing their invasion from underneath the door and marching up the kitchen cupboards before disappearing somewhere behind the pile of dirty dishes in the sink – the dishes' shape mirroring the outline of the mountain range that was barely visible in the distance through the windows. Charlie's fan droned on. Rotating from side to side, it created a polished semi-circle on the otherwise dusty and sandy floor. The fridge's motor kicked in with a rattle, and then belched out a continuous electrical hum.

I touched my forehead with my fingertips, and was surprised to find that I had neither hangover nor headache. The room was already hot and stuffy, and I could feel the intensity of the sun trying to force its way through the closed shutters on the window above me. My watch read 11:13. It was my first full eight hours' sleep in a long time, and I felt better for it. Images of the previous night flashed through my mind, and I winced. No matter, despite all the drama, I felt liberated and revived.

The door creaked open, and Charlie stepped in. 'How's the patient?' he asked.

'Not too bad.'

'Hannah's outside looking for a re-match.'

'What?'

'Only joking,' he laughed. 'She actually feels pretty shit about it.'

'I probably deserved it though.'

'Maybe,' he said, looking around the room. I followed his gaze.

'So what's the plan for today?' I asked.

'The wedding's on.'

'Shit, I forgot. What does that mean?'

'It means free grub and free booze till the wee hours of the morning.'

I looked around the room again. 'I think I'm going to give this place a tidy,' I said. 'Sort my clothes out and get a bit organised. I'm still taking stuff out of my bag, and I've already been here a week.'

'Feels longer though doesn't it?'

I nodded. It felt like a month.

'The wedding's not till this afternoon,' he said. 'We're going over to the pool for a bit. Fancy coming?'

'No, I think I'm going to do a bit of a clean-up. I'll join you later.'

'Okay. Suit yourself, mate. Talk to you later.' He left, grabbing the towel that was hanging on one of the wardrobe doors. The door creaked again, and he was gone. I heard their voices fading further away and lay there listening to the fridge and the fan operating in electrical unison.

Capitalising on my good mood, I found a Rolling Stones' Greatest Hits cassette tape, and, for the next hour, Mick Jagger, Keith Richards and the other two motivated me into action. I swept, washed and tidied and even cleaned up the empty cans, bottles and cigarette butts lying on the ground outside the room. I was sitting in the sun, reading *Catch-22* and sipping on a mug of tea when Aengus and Charlie arrived back.

Both headed inside for a siesta before the wedding. After my marathon sleep, I decided to stay outside in the sun. On the almost two hours expended on cleaning the room, only Aengus passed a comment.

'Hey, Joe,' he yelled at me, sticking his head out the door. 'Where'd you put my alarm clock?'

The Syndicate of 'M&M Enterprises' was being carefully explained to Yossarian in *Catch-22* when an ominous shadow loomed over me, thereby darkening the pages of my book. I squinted up at the figure, the sun beaming just above her shoulders. At first, I thought it was M, and I smiled.

'Hi,' I said. 'How are you?'

Her head moved into the path of the sun and I saw that it was Hannah. My expression must have changed as she said: 'Were you expecting someone else?'

'No,' I stuttered. 'I wasn't...'

'Listen,' she interrupted me, 'I'm sorry about last night. I don't know what got hold of me.'

'I probably deserved it.'

'Yes,' she said. 'You deserved it, but that's not the point. It was stupid of me. I'm not normally the jealous type. It's just that I...' She stopped. I looked up at her, unsure of what to say.

'I'm sorry,' she blurted out, as if pulling off a plaster from a wound.

'I'm sorry too,' I said.

She stuck her hand out uncomfortably towards me, and I took it.

'You're still an *arschloch*,' she smiled, and I smiled back at her.

I raised my hand to block out the sun, as I watched her walk away.

The wedding was due to start at four. Aengus, Charlie and myself had made a bit of an effort by wearing long-sleeved shirts. I had found an old iron in one of the wardrobes during my clean up, and we had taken turns using a towel and the hard marble floor as an improvised ironing board.

On the main lawn where Itai and I had carelessly scattered the tables and chairs the previous day, an inviting banquet was now laid out for about four hundred people. White tablecloths covered every table, each one set for eight people. The cobblelock area at the edge of the lawn was dominated by a large stage, professionally assembled with lights, microphones and a backdrop. Four long tables on each side were laid out in a rectangular shape. On each table was an array of empty stainless steel trays waiting to be filled with food.

The atmosphere was warm and relaxed. Some people sat at their assigned table and chatted. Others sauntered about smiling. Occasionally, a person dressed in their blue work clothes, would rush by carrying a tray or heading to attend to some electrical fault. A bar had been set up in the corner for use later that night. Soft Israeli folk songs from tall speakers filled the air as children played games around the stage. The six giant Hebrew letters *Mazal Tov* (Congratulations) were now decorated with various coloured light bulbs. Eventually, just after four, people took their seats, and the music stopped. I looked around for M and saw her seated with her family, talking to her mother. We were the first of the volunteers to arrive, so Charlie went off to find our table. I stood and looked over at M's table while I waited.

She was wearing a light white dress and wore her hair long and loose over her shoulders. At first, I didn't think anything about the procession of people arriving at her table every minute or so, and kissing her on each cheek. It was a wedding. Generally, people get to meet people they haven't seen in a while. Wasn't that supposed to be one of the best, or worse, outcomes of attending a wedding in the first place? After I observed the fourth such interaction, I guessed that M was related to either the bride or the groom. Strangely, none of the other members of her family ever stood up during these proceedings, or was greeted separately. Like condensation slowly clearing from a car windscreen, it slowly dawned on me.

'Fuck,' I said to myself but loud enough that one or two people around me looked over in my direction. It was her birthday. It was her birthday today. Sixteen. What an idiot. How could I have forgotten? And even worse, what the hell was I supposed to get her at this late stage. Would the colbo be open today? Of course not. What the hell could I buy in there for her anyway? Shampoo? A multi-pack of chewing gum? How could I have forgotten?

'Hey, you okay?' Charlie asked.

'What?'

'You look a little agitated. Everything okay?'

'Yeah, yeah. I'm okay, thanks,' I said.

'Our table's over here.' I followed Charlie and Aengus to a table, which was, as ever, near the back and furthest away from the stage.

'Are you okay, mate?' Charlie asked me again when we were seated. I was chewing my fingernails.

'Is the colbo open today?'

'Of course not,' he said. 'Why? Do you need something?'

'It's ah...' I said looking over at M.

'What?' he asked me, following my stare.

I leaned into him.

'It's a little... well it's a little embarrassing actually.'

'Oh, I see,' he said. 'Listen don't worry about it, mate. I've got some in my room.'

'What?'

'You don't have to buy them here,' he said. 'I told you they're free.'

'What are you talking about?' I asked him and then I realised what he was talking about. 'No, no. That's not what I mean. I need to get a birthday present for M. It's her birthday today.'

'Oh right. How old is she then? Twelve?'

'She's sixteen, you prick, and you know it.'

He looked over at her. 'Sweet sixteen,' he said and licked his lips.

'Forget about it,' I said, getting annoyed.

'No, no,' he laughed. 'I'm just fucking with you, mate.'

'Well, I'm not in the mood.'

'What do you need?'

'A shop would help,' I answered. 'When's the next bus to Beersheba?'

'About seven o'clock this evening. It's the Shabbat so there aren't any buses till sunset. An hour there. An hour back. You just might make it back in time for last orders.'

I considered this.

'There's always the Kfar,' Charlie added.

'What's that?'

'It's the university town across the desert.'

'And there's a shop there?'

'Yeah, but it's more of a mini-market. There's a cafe there as well.'

'Why isn't it closed today if it's a holy day?' I asked him.

'Don't know to be honest. Maybe 'cause it's a university town and the students need the shop.'

'You sure it's open?'

'Yeah,' he said. 'Aengus and I have gone over a couple of times on a Saturday just for something to do.'

'Okay, thanks,' I said and stood up.

'What? You're not going are you?'

'Yep.'

'Now?'

'Why not?'

'Because the wedding's about to start.'

I looked over at the stage. In a small group of trees to one side, I saw that the bride and groom were waiting. I looked down at Charlie and shrugged.

'It's not my wedding, mate,' I told him.

'It's a bit of a walk.'

'How long?'

'A good hour at least.'

As everyone was seated, I crouched down and made my way away from the tables but then turned back and slipped into my seat again.

'In which direction?' I asked Charlie, and he smiled at me.

He told me that just down from the volunteers' houses there was a gap in the fence which I needed to crawl through. From outside the kibbutz fence, I then had to walk straight on for at least thirty minutes until I came to a five-hundred-foot drop into a canyon. From there, I was to turn right and follow along the edge of the canyon for another thirty minutes or so. By then, I'd have reached the edge of the university campus. Someone would direct me from there.

As I left the wedding, the music got underway, and I caught a peek of the bride and groom as they made their way to the stage. Back in my room, I switched my shoes for trainers, grabbed whatever shekels I had (one hundred and thirty nine) and went looking for the gap in the fence. I found it easily, but as I was crawling through, I caught my trousers on a sharp wire. When I tried to free myself, the wire dug into a calf muscle and sliced open my skin. I let out an involuntary yell. I sat down to look at the damage and saw a cut about the size and width of a matchstick. Blood was oozing out, but the cut wasn't all that deep, so I decided to carry on.

Although the heat of the sun was beginning to dwindle, it was still quite warm. I was already sweating and thirsty by the time I reached the canyon, where I could see an immense valley stretching from one side to the other. Subsequently, I was told that if I followed the canyon for twenty miles west, I would find myself in Egypt; thirty miles to the east and I would be in Jordan. For the moment though I was happy to concentrate my efforts on the mini-market another thirty minutes away. I stayed as close to the edge of the cliff as possible and could already see the cluster of buildings that marked the outskirts of the university campus. I checked my watch; it was five o'clock. The wedding ceremony was probably over by now and they would be serving the meal.

For no particular reason, thoughts of my friends back in Dublin came into my mind. If they were to see me at that moment, what would they think? How would I explain to them where I was or what I was doing? Over the next few years, I would find myself in many strange situations – moments that were as strange to my old life, as my friends would consider my new life here in Israel to be right now.

In the years that followed, I often tried to explain or describe the many bizarre circumstances I found myself in, to share these crests of adventure in their otherwise smooth lives, for them to see the world from my point of view. To explain. To demonstrate. To illustrate.

Inevitably, this would prove pointless. They would listen with an impatient politeness, and soon I would sound as if I was bragging. Perhaps I was. Or perhaps I needed them as witnesses to my experiences – in order to make them more real to me. Conversations would quickly return to a more local or current event. To onlookers, I would appear to be sharing a private joke with myself – a joke that only I understood. I learned that these private memories and moments should always remain sacred and personal; that they never can and never should be shared. Like friends from work and lifelong friends, each set has their place, and the two very rarely mix well together.

I had been walking for over an hour by the time I reached the perimeter fence of the Kfar. There were huge gaps all along the fence, so I got in easily enough. There was no one around. The buildings were similar to those in our kibbutz, but they were surrounded by less greenery and vegetation. It reminded me of one of those abandoned towns in 1950s Arizona where they used to test the effects of nuclear bombs. I walked around for about ten minutes; the only living thing I saw was a dog, which paid no attention to me. It was only by sheer fluke that I walked down an alley, which opened up into a courtyard, on the far side of which was a cafe with outdoor seating. It had no staff and no customers. Alongside the building on my left were some colourful signs which seemed to be advertising chocolate or ice cream. I saw the darkness in the shop even before I saw the shutters pulled down over the door. I was too late. I cupped my hands to the glass to see inside, but there was no one there. I felt absolutely gutted.

The sound of a door slamming echoed through the small courtyard. Keys rattled in a lock. I ran around the back of the shop and there was a stout, middle-aged woman with jet-black hair walking away from the door.

'No, wait, wait,' I called out to her.

She stopped and turned around to face me.

'I need to get something from the shop.'

'It closed,' she said and walked away.

'No, wait please,' I said. 'It'll only take me a minute. I promise.'

She didn't stop walking. 'I say it closed.'

I ran in front of her and placed the palms of my hands together like a good Catholic. 'Please. Two minutes. I'll only take two minutes.'

She made a guttural sort of a sound and stepped around me. I ran in front of her and took out whatever money I had. She stopped.

'Please?' I pleaded again, holding out the money. I took a twenty-shekel note and offered it to her. 'I'll only be two minutes, I promise.'

She ignored the twenty shekels I proffered, and instead reached for my other hand and took a fifty-shekel note. She began mumbling in Hebrew but turned around and headed back towards the shop. I followed her with my now eighty-nine shekels.

It was after seven-thirty when I finally arrived back to the kibbutz. The remaining daylight was fading fast as I crawled back under the fence. I could hear the loud music coming from the wedding party on the lawn. My excursion proved to be a tougher ordeal than I had anticipated, and I needed to freshen up. The heat from the shower opened up the wound on my leg and turned the water to a shade of light red. Dressed in a fresh T-shirt, I made my way back to the wedding, carrying a small blue plastic bag, which held M's gift from the Kfar. I went over to the volunteers' table. Aengus and Guy were arm wrestling each other, and everyone else seemed to be placing bets on which of them would win. Apparently, the free bar had been a great success. Charlie was refereeing the duel, crouched down on his knees watching the pair's elbows. I wanted to ask him if he had seen M but now didn't look like a good time to pose such a question.

I went over to the stage where people were dancing to a fast Israeli pop song. I had an overview of the entire party from this standpoint. The table where M had been sitting was now empty. I searched around for some friends of hers that I'd seen her with earlier that week, but I couldn't spot her anywhere.

Aengus had won the arm wrestle and was limbering up his hand in preparation for the next challenger – Hannah. Charlie was taking bets from everyone's pink cards.

'Charlie,' I called to him, raising my voice above the music.

'Hey, Joseph,' he called back. 'You made it.'

'Have you seen M?'

'Olga, you can't bet ten shekels, you've only got seven on your card,' he shouted at her.

'Charlie,' I tried again. 'Have you seen M?'

'No. No, I haven't.'

'Shit,' I said.

'Chad, are you betting on this one?' Charlie asked, and then turned to me. 'Go over and ask Dafna where she is'

'Which one is Dafna?'

'The girl that sits with us sometimes in the dining room. Her parents are American, so her English is good.'

'Can I trust her?' I asked him, but his attention was turned back to Hannah as she placed her elbow on the table. I walked around the tables looking for Dafna. Everyone was in great form and a part of me wished I could join in. I promised myself that if Dafna said that M had gone home, as disappointed as I knew I would be, I would forget about her for the night and go back and enjoy the rest of the evening with the other volunteers.

I soon found Dafna sitting with a bunch of other girls. She saw me and, intuitively, as women often are, she stood up and came over to me.

'Hi,' she said to me, as American and as effervescent as Minnie Mouse.

'Hello. I'm Joseph.'

'Yeah, I know,' she said. 'Hi.'

'I was wondering...'

'She's not here.'

'Who?'

'M.'

'How do you know...?' I asked her but decided that I'd rather not know.

'She said she wasn't feeling well,' Dafna said.

'Oh right. Will she be back?'

'I don't know. Sorry.'

'No, it's okay. Thanks for telling me,' I said and turned to walk away.

'She was looking for you though,' Dafna called after me.

'Was she?' I asked.

'Yep. If I see her I'll tell her you were looking for her too.'

'Thanks,' I said but must have sounded a bit sullen.

'Don't worry,' she said. 'She's looking for you and you're looking for her. You're both bound to bump into one another.'

She smiled at me and went back to her friends.

I walked over to the bar and ordered a Goldstar, determined to put M out of my mind for the night. Back at the volunteers' table Hannah was in the winner's seat, and Shir was sitting opposite her. Aengus was sitting on his own, looking surly. I stood at the edge of the group for a moment looking on. A wave of melancholy swept over me; I tried to fight it but I couldn't. Suddenly, I felt quite despondent – disappointed at how the evening had turned out, disappointment in myself. I looked down at the fresh cold beer in my hand and then up at my new friends having a great time together. I wanted so much to join them, but knew that I couldn't. I had known M for only a few days, and I already missed her. Wherever she was on the kibbutz at that moment, she was only a few minutes' walk away, but she might as well have been as far away as a trek along the canyon to Egypt or Jordan. I placed the full glass of beer on the table beside me, stood up and made my way back to my room.

As I approached the volunteers' houses, I changed my mind about brooding in my room alone. It was a warm night and it would be much more agreeable to sulk under the stars. My head was much too full of thoughts to be contained in a single, small, sultry room, so instead I wandered along empty paths and allowed my desires and longings to find their own way into the night sky, releasing me from their burden. Unfortunately, however, as one thought escaped, another appeared and took its place. I walked aimlessly for about ten minutes and eventually found myself outside the pub and the disco. The buildings stood silently, in contrast to the previous evening. I touched the side of my jaw unconsciously, then turned and walked back towards the members' houses, only the moon and the stars lighting my way. I passed rows of olive trees, the celestial light turning their leaves silver and making the ripe olives sparkle like pearls between the branches. Turning left, I found myself on the outer road passing a derelict allotment of dead scrub and plants. Just ahead of me was a collection of four wooden prefabs, each with a decking area, part of which was fashioned into a front porch. I guessed that the wooden buildings were used for storage purposes, as they were in complete darkness, and looked quite rundown and untidy.

From the corner of my eye, I saw something move on the porch of the second prefab. I continued walking eyes straining, thinking it may be a wild dog. I spotted another movement, bigger this time, so I quickened my pace and turned in the opposite direction.

'Joseph?' someone called out.

I stopped and looked over.

'M?' I asked.

She emerged from the shadow of the building, walking towards me. 'What are you doing here?' I asked her.

'What are you doing here?' she asked me.

'I got bored at the wedding and came for a walk. Dafna told me you weren't feeling well and had gone home.'

'I drank some wine for my birthday, and I think I drink too much. I felt not so good. I went home, but then instead decided to walk.'

'How are you now?' I asked.

'Good. Thank you. I looked for you.'

'Yes, Dafna told me.'

'She tells you a lot,' she said smiling.

I smiled back at her, and we looked at each other for a few moments.

'Do you want to come sit with me?' she asked. I followed her back to the porch, and we sat in silence for a while.

'So, do you come here often?' I asked.

'What do you mean?'

'Nothing,' I said. 'Just a bad joke.'

'Ah, I see. And do you know any good jokes?'

I thought for a moment. I could hear the music from the wedding.

'Oh, right. I got one. Did you hear about the two antennas that met on a roof and got married?'

'Antennas?'

'Aerials,' I explained.

'Oh, I see. And they got married?'

'Yes.'

'Is that the joke?'

'No. They got married, and I went to their wedding.'

'You did?'

'No, it's the joke.'

'I don't get it.'

'It's not over yet. They got married, and I went to their wedding. Wait,' I said holding up my hand. 'The wedding was awful but afterwards there was a great reception.'

I looked at her, and she blinked once.

'Is it finished?' she asked.

'Yes, thankfully,' I said and leaned back against the wall. We sat facing out onto the derelict area with the olive trees in the background.

'I had a nice time yesterday,' she said.

'So did I.'

'Why did you not go to the wedding today?'

'Oh, I forgot,' I said and sat up, turning to face her. I was still holding the folded-up blue plastic bag in my hand. 'I went to get you a gift for your birthday.'

'Today?'

'Yeah.'

'Where?'

'The Kfar.'

'You walked over there today?'

'It didn't take that long,' I said looking down and opening the bag. I could feel her staring at me.

'Okay,' I said rummaging away. 'Now don't get too excited. It wasn't as interesting a shop as I had hoped for.'

'Should I close my eyes?'

'I think it'll be easier to hide your disappointment if you just keep them open.'

We were both kneeling, facing each other.

'So,' I said. 'Gift number one...'

'There's more than one gift?' she asked and held out her hand.

'Gift number one is...' I said, and placed the item in her hand.

She looked down at it. 'This is my favourite type of chewing gum,' she said.

'I knew that,' I smiled. 'Also, if you look closely, you'll see that it's a double pack.'

'Wow. I'm impressed.'

'Good,' I said. 'Now for gift number two.'

She held out her hand again.

'So hard to buy something for the girl who has everything,' I said and placed the gift in her hand. She looked down at it. Then looked up at me.

'But I don't smoke,' she said.

'Yes, I know, but it's not just an ordinary cigarette lighter. Look,' I said and turned it on. 'It's wind-resistant. It'll never blow out in the wind.'

I blew on it. It went out.

'Well, maybe not a strong wind,' I conceded.

'Well, if I ever think about smoking,' she said, 'it will be very useful. On a non-windy day maybe.'

'It also has a lifetime guarantee.'

'Perhaps then I could keep it if I ever have children, and they want to smoke.'

'That's a lovely thought,' I said laughing.

'But you smoke. Why don't you use it till then?'

'But I bought it for you.'

'Yes, but this way I get a birthday gift, and you get a lighter.'

'That makes perfect sense,' I said. 'Plus, I've always wanted a lighter with a lifetime guarantee.'

'But remember, if you smoke, then your life will be shorter. So is the guarantee for your life or for mine?'

I took the lighter from her hand and put it into my pocket. 'I'll have a smoke later and think about that one.'

I reached into the bag again. 'And finally,' I said. 'A birthday card.'

She took it and opened the envelope. She looked at the cover.

'Why Happy Anniversary?' she asked.

'What?'

'The card says "Happy Anniversary".'

'Oh shit,' I said. 'The shop assistant wasn't the most helpful person in the world.'

She opened the card and read out loud...

'"*Dear M, I do not know what the next twenty, thirty or forty years will have in store for me. But whatever fortune or misfortune, I know, without doubt, that I will always remember watching the sunset over the desert with the most beautiful and wonderful girl I have ever met. And that even when I am an old man, it will always make me smile. Happy Birthday. Your friend, Joseph.*"'

She looked up at me. '*Toda raba,*' she said. 'That's really very nice.'

A loud cheer went up from the wedding party in the distance, and the music changed to a much faster and more modern beat. She looked over her shoulder in its direction.

'Should we get back?' I asked.

'Yes, I suppose so.'

'Can I see you again?'

'Yes.'

'When?'

'Tomorrow. Here. At eight.'

'Is it allowed that we see each other?'

'Allowed by the kibbutz?' she asked. 'In the army they have what is known as the kit bag question. Do you know what this is?'

'No.'

'It is when the commander tells the soldier to run ten times around the camp. And the new soldier asks – "Do I have to run with my kit bag?" and the commander tells him, "Yes, now you have to". Understand?'

'Okay,' I said.

She stood up and patted the dust off her clothes, and I did the same.

'Thank you for the gifts and the card,' she said, and extended her arms for a hug.

We hugged, the sides of our faces touching. We held onto each other for a few moments, and then I pulled my head up and looked into her brown eyes. I leaned forward and kissed her, and she pressed into me. I pulled away from her and touched her face. She smiled up at me, and then leaned forward again, this time deeper into each other.

The same song continued to play, and I silently prayed that it would never end.

12

Like a train pulling out slowly from a railway station, the first week had crept along. Everything and everyone was different and in contrast to everything I'd known or experienced up to that point in my life. Almost every moment was alive and fully lived, and sometimes even radiated with the strangeness and the excitement of the new. Charlie's observation was prescient however. Soon, the weeks began to merge into one another and then became blurred as they passed me by as stoically as time itself, flicking away like the pages of a book caught in a gust of wind.

The following morning, I was back in front of the dishwasher. While Sunday was the first day of the working week, I never had that 'Monday morning' feeling that I had always dreaded when I was working in Dublin. Quite often in the kibbutz, I would start work at six in the morning on a Sunday, knowing that at the very same moment it was exactly four o'clock in the morning in Dublin and many of my friends would be just on the point of climbing into bed after a Saturday night's drinking and gallivanting. I can't say, however, that I ever felt cheated on that score.

This particular morning I was feeling euphoric as a result of the previous evening's events and, for a moment, I had almost convinced myself that I had dreamt up the whole thing when I suddenly caught sight of M, and she waved over at me. I played a tape by Thin Lizzy loudly on the stereo and sang along blissfully. It seemed though that I was alone in my bliss. For the rest of the kibbutz – the wedding having continued on until late into the night, or rather that morning – everything was moving in slow motion and as noiselessly as possible. A collective hangover had settled over the kibbutz like a dark shroud. The music in the kitchen was low and lazy, and the usual cackle emanating from the soldier girls had quelled to a series of monosyllabic grunts. Charlie pushed buckets about in a zombie-like fashion and more often than not could be found sitting (or hiding) on the bottom step outside, holding a cup of coffee and staring into the distance.

Aengus was worse. When I met him at lunchtime, he looked like he still hadn't been to bed, and I strongly suspected he was still drunk. News had come through that the expected Swedish group had cancelled their trip due to the possibility of war breaking out in the very near future. He was furious. Nobody else seemed to care that much, with the exception of Jenny, who looked very pleased. I had forgotten about the impending war and now I wondered how it would affect me, but since no one knew what was going to happen, or when it was likely to happen, my thoughts soon drifted back to M. Itai came in and told me he had asked Rosa if I could help him the following day. He'd been instructed earlier on that day to bring all the tables and chairs back to their storage area and he had refused to do it without some help.

After work, I followed Charlie and Aengus over to the swimming pool.

'So, what's the difference then between MI6 and an M16?' Aengus was asking Guy.

'Jesus, I've told you already,' Guy answered, infuriated. 'MI6 is your version of the CIA and an M16 is a machine gun.'

'So who are the FBI, then?' asked Aengus.

'The FBI is like your MI5 in Britain. Christ, Aengus, how do you not know this?'

'The FBI is like MI5? And MI6 is like the CIA? So what the fuck's an F16?'

'It's a fucking plane, you moron. Christ, I'm going for a swim,' Guy said, standing up. I saw Aengus wink at Charlie as he stormed off.

'And to what do we owe this honour?' Aengus asked, turning to me. I hadn't spent that much time with the two of them since I'd arrived the previous week, so I didn't think the remark was too harsh.

'Do you have any suncream, now that you're here?' he asked me.

I told him that I didn't.

'Ah, of course you dinnae,' he said. 'Just like Charlie boy here. Sure why would you two need suncream anyway when all you ever do is the girlie jobs?'

He reached over and unfolded his towel and then placed it full length over his body. 'Hey Charlie,' he said as he closed his eyes. 'Wake me up if Jenny comes over in that wee white bikini, will ye?'

'Don't be playing with yourself under that towel,' Charlie replied, but Aengus was already half asleep.

I swam a few lengths of the pool. When I got out, Shir and Chad were sitting with Charlie.

'Jesus,' Guy said to me. 'You're probably the whitest guy I've ever seen.'

'He's right,' Charlie said. 'You Celts just can't take the sun.'

He stood up and walked over to Aengus who lay unconscious on the grass. Very gently, he raised the towel off him and threw it in a heap on the grass beside him. The others sniggered.

'Ouch,' Shir said. 'That's probably not a good idea.'

'That's all right,' Charlie replied. 'I've had worse ideas.'

'You're the one who's going to have to listen to him bitch later,' Guy said.

'It'll be worth it,' Charlie said and sat back in the shade. 'He never stops bitching either way.'

I could almost hear Aengus's skin start to sizzle, like frying bacon.

In the furthest corner away from the pool, Itai and a few other soldiers sat on deckchairs in the shade drinking beers and smoking. I went over to them and asked Itai for suncream. He said he didn't have any.

'What's the name of that girl who works in the factory?' I asked him.

'Which one?'

'The dark-haired one over there, near the gate.'

'Einav.'

'I'll ask her,' I said. 'Does she speak English?'

'I don't know.'

'What's suncream in Hebrew?'

'*Mitz cuz*,' he replied. I'd heard the word *mitz* being used in the dining room several times and knew that it meant juice. Perhaps, I thought, this language wasn't so difficult after all.

I wondered later though why, when Itai had said *mitz cuz*, none of the other guys had laughed or even flinched. He'd said it as if it was the most natural thing in the world. Of course, when I asked Einav if I could have some of her *mitz cuz*, she'd turned the brightest of reds, saw Itai and his friends laughing hysterically, naturally assumed that I knew exactly what I had just asked her for, grabbed her towel, picked up all her things and left. Apparently *mitz* does indeed mean juice, however *cuz* is something entirely different.

I went along to supper in the dining room later that evening. I'd had a difficult time with the food over the previous week but, finally, my innards were beginning to make sense of the Middle Eastern cuisine. I was quite sure that the onslaught of salads could only be having a positive effect on my well-being, long term. Unfortunately, however, the banal ubiquity of the salads mixed with copious amounts of beer, coffee and cigarettes in the short term at least, was proving to be an intestinal challenge. I had suffered a mild case of Delhi Belly which, I was later informed, was common among new arrivals in the kibbutz. Sparing you the details, but it seemed to have worked its way out of my system, quite literally.

I passed the public phone box on my way to meet M. I hadn't called home in almost a week and now I was procrastinating for yet another day as I made my way to the prefabs. I got there a little early but she was already there, waiting in the shadows. We talked easily, falling silent whenever someone walked by on the path near us. It felt good being hidden, unseen by passersby, wrapped in the darkness with my beautiful and somewhat illicit prize. We talked about everything and nothing, and time stood still with only our breathing as witnesses to its passing. But, time cheated us when we weren't paying attention, and suddenly it was ten o'clock.

'What about me taking you to dinner some evening in Beersheba?' I asked her, as she was about to say goodnight.

'Where could we go?'

'I've no idea,' I said. 'I've only been there once, and that was for about thirty minutes. So, unless you fancy eating from a takeaway stand in the bus station, I'm afraid you'll have to decide where we go.'

'Okay. We'll go after *Rosh hashannah.*'

'What's that?'

'New Year's Day.'

'Shit,' I said. 'I was hoping it could be a bit sooner than that.'

'It's not so far away.'

'Okay, but if you fancy going before then, let me know.'

'I can wait,' she said, and we kissed again and said goodnight.

She left first, and then I slowly walked back to my room in the opposite direction smoking and smiling.

The next morning, as I hung onto the side of the trailer while Itai drove the tractor, our routine almost seemed like the most natural thing in the world. We had done our morning tour and clean-up of the kibbutz, and we were now heading back out to the desert to dump the bits and pieces we'd collected. The trench was much fuller than the previous time I'd been there. Huge branches and plants spilled out over the sides. We needed to drive around the back in order to find room for our rubbish.

'Fucking *Noy,*' (Garden Department) Itai said. Apparently, the guys in charge of the gardens had cut down some trees the afternoon before and had dumped them all here. We drove back to our shed close to the dining room, where the tractor was normally parked after work each day. Itai unlocked the door, went in and brought out a petrol canister. We drove to the back of the garage, filled it up with petrol, and then headed back out to the desert. He jumped off the tractor, doused the trees and our accumulation of rubbish with the petrol, and then took out his Zippo. Lighting a cigarette first, he then bent down and pulled out a piece of paper from between the branches. He lit the paper, watched it ignite, and then threw it into the dump. He turned away and walked towards me. The earth that had been taken out of the ground to make the trench was piled high, and I was standing on top of it. The petrol caught on fire and spread quickly through the rubbish, dry scrub and tumbleweed underneath. Itai didn't turn around as the flames shot up into the air. A harsh yellow and orange glow exploded into the blue sky as he took a drag from his cigarette.

He climbed the small mound, and we sat and watched the flames. After a few minutes the flames spread out further along the trench and soon reached close to us. With the soaring heat from the sun above and the raw intensity of the billowing flames surging towards us, the heat intensified, and I stood up uncomfortably.

'What's next?' I asked him. He took out a little notebook from his pocket and flicked through the pages.

'Golda wants some mousetraps,' he said standing up. We walked back towards the tractor, him in front of me, but he suddenly stopped and looked back towards the dump. The fire was quite strong now. I followed the direction of his concerned expression but couldn't see anything.

'What is it?' I asked. He raised his head into the air like a dog and sniffed.

'Do you smell it?' he asked me, but I wasn't sure what particular smell he was talking about; there were so many different smells in the air because there were so many different things on fire. He walked past me, trying to get as close as possible to the flames. I followed him, protecting my face from the heat using my arm, but this merely resulted in my arm taking the brunt of the heat.

He stopped at one particular point and looked down. By the time I was standing beside him, I could smell it. I was a musky yet putrid smell – sweet yet vile.

'Look,' he said, pointing into the fire with one hand and covering his mouth and nose with the other. I tried to adjust my eyes to the twirling flames as they danced around like taunting devils in the hole. Eventually, I could make out what looked like a large leather bag, the flames massaging its every side.

'Jesus,' I said. 'What the hell is that?'

'A sheep,' he mumbled through his hand.

Almost as he said it, what must have been its stomach or its liver or its heart for all I knew, exploded. The fire hissed in protest, and up shot an acidic smell that turned us on our heels. I almost gagged into the sand. Unbelievably, I was still holding my cigarette, which I flung away in disgust.

'You okay?' Itai asked me.

'Who put that there?'

'Probably some Bedouin,' he said. 'It must have died, and he hid it there so that he wouldn't have to get rid of it.'

A couple of weeks later in the dining room, someone put out their cigarette by shoving it into the side of the half-eaten chicken on their plate. The acerbic smell emitted, as the cigarette was extinguished, reminded me of the smell that day. There are many smells that are similar to the smell of burning skin, but none are quite as unique.

We headed back and parked the tractor; Itai unlocked the door of the little shed and emerged with the mousetraps for Golda. They consisted of rectangular-shaped trays made of Styrofoam, about the size of a thin paperback novel. On one side was a sticky substance, which was baited with cheese or jam or whatever was going. Itai claimed that his pita bread worked best.

'I need to talk to Golda about *Rosh hashannah*,' he said. 'Will you wait for me outside the storeroom?'

'*Rosh hashannah*?' I asked. 'You mean the New Year? It's a bit early, isn't it?'

'It's this Thursday,'

'What?'

'The Jewish New Year. Not 1991.'

'Oh, I see,' I said. 'That's great.' I immediately started to plan a night out with M. After a few minutes, Itai came down with the new mousetraps and the key for the storeroom.

'I shouldn't have asked her,' Itai complained. 'She gave me a whole list of shit she wants.'

'That means you'll need me again tomorrow.'

'Okay, I'll mention it to Rosa later.'

'Great,' I said.

The storeroom, cool inside, was almost in complete darkness. Itai turned on the lights and removed a new bin liner from the wall. He opened up the new mousetraps and put bits of pita in the centre of each one. He explained that the mouse would attempt to walk across the sticky side to get to the bait and would then get stuck there. I didn't really give this concept too much thought until he lifted a wooden crate to reveal the location of the first trap. There I could see three mice trapped. The first one lay dead in the centre of the mousetrap. The second one lay closer to the edge. Obviously, it had been more determined than the first mouse to reach the food; it had struggled so much with the exertion that even after its feet had become stuck, it had succeeded in ripping open its own body with the effort. The third mouse was still alive, twitching and struggling to free itself. The whole thing was covered in mouse shit. Without a word, Itai picked it up, folded the mousetrap in half, placed it on the floor, and hammered it using his right foot. There was the simultaneous sound of a faint squeak and a squishy splat.

He uncovered the other four mousetraps that he'd hidden the previous time and replaced them with new ones. The last one held about ten mice, some of them babies. I was amazed at how the mice apparently crawled over the dead ones whose little corpses were already torn open, in order to get at the food. I said this to Itai and he proudly told me it was because his pita was so good.

A few months after that, I became responsible for replacing the traps on my own. I didn't have the nerve or courage to stomp on the still half-alive mice, so I decided to drown them instead. This feeble attempt at offering them a more humane death was actually just my squeamishness in disguise. It involved placing the bin liner opening under a tap and then sealing the bag. This was all working out pretty well until a mouse stuck his head out from underneath one of the Styrofoam trays and tried to raise his head above the rising water level. I could see him desperately fighting for his last few breaths, looking up in my direction, as the weight of his dead comrades on the tray pulled him back down under the water.

After that, I found that if I imagined I was merely dealing with some rotten fruit, the stomping wasn't so bad.

As I had some time before heading over to M that evening, I thought it best to take the opportunity to phone home. Sometimes, being so far away from home felt almost like I was living someone else's life. I never did anything out of character, but I certainly felt more of an acceptance and impartiality to almost everything that would have been impossible at home. A ceiling of inevitability was completely removed and behavioural expectations were lost.

At home everyone was concerned about reports of the massive build-up of American troops in Saudi Arabia. Television news footage showed Saddam Hussein with a frightened little five-year-old English boy who had been kidnapped along with his family. Newspapers showed maps of the Middle East indicating how far Iraqi weapons could reach; where I was located was well within that range. There was much talk of chemical weapons and the horrific implications of such use. When my family looked at these maps, all they saw was the presumed proximity of my desert home to Iraq. When I looked at the desert, all I saw was sand and chicken houses. My foremost thoughts were always about M; leaving Israel was never even an option. I did my best to sound unconcerned and to convince my parents that they had nothing to worry about, but I always ended up sounding puerile and flippant.

In my defence, I honestly thought that the whole thing would blow over. It wouldn't be the first time that I was completely wrong about something.

Apparently, kids in Jewish schools are taught that BC, where it refers to a particular date, means 'Before Counting'. I thought this strange since both BC and AD are both named after a Jew. I informed M what BC and AD actually meant, but to be fair they have been counting the years a lot longer than Christians have. In the Jewish calendar 1990 was actually 5751.

The literal translation of *Rosh hashannah* is 'head of the year'. It is one of the High Holidays in Judaism, one of the 'Days of Awe', but for us volunteers it meant nothing more than a day off work. The dining room was laid out as if for a Sabbath meal on a Friday; there was much emphasis on honey, apples and the blowing of some sort of animal horn. My absolute ignorance of Jewish holidays and their various meanings still surprises me, even after spending so many years in Israel. I suppose I'd learned so much about the many traditions of Catholicism that I was loath to learn yet another new set.

The following week, there was a party planned in the volunteers' bomb shelter, and I brought M back to my room for the first time. My version of a quick clean-up was shoving Aengus's, Charlie's and my own stuff under our respective beds. Charlie came into the room to get more beers from the fridge and he was as charming to her as only true Englishmen can be. M too reciprocated in her charming way; and after Charlie left, she made me tea recalling exactly how I liked it. She handed it to me, kissed me, and then took out a large chocolate bar and broke it in two, giving me the biggest piece. We sipped our tea and listened to the lugubrious lyrics of Leonard Cohen. As I sat watching her delicately chewing on the chocolate, she turned and smiled at me, and I felt my heart surrender to her, and the room and the world stayed exactly as it had always been, but everything in my world was irrevocably changed forever.

One Friday I borrowed an electric hair cutter from Markus. I spent about twenty minutes clipping and cutting and was very proud of the results. I was finishing up and thought I looked almost civilised when Guy came into the room. He seemed impressed with the machine and asked to borrow it, but I told him that since it belonged to Markus, I'd need to get his permission first. He played with it for a minute or two and then left. I got off the bed and looked in the mirror again. I thought one side of my hair was slightly uneven, so I plugged in the cutter once again. I hadn't noticed that Guy had been messing with the adjustments, so when I ran it through the right hand side of my head, the resulting effect was like that of a lawnmower demolishing high grass. I was left with a bald white strip that looked like a concrete runway in the middle of the Amazon forest. A rush of anger at Guy, and at myself, convulsed me to such an extent that I started to shave off the rest of my hair. Wads of dark hair fell to the ground until I was left with nothing but a clump of hair on the back of my head only.

With the front part of my head looking as bald as Sinead O'Connor and the back part looking as hairy as Hazel O'Connor, I went in search of someone to finish off the job, but not before grabbing a cold beer to drown my sorrows. I found Olga sunbathing and she obliged me. Charlie came back from the pool to find Olga dressed in a bikini bending over me, a beer in my hand, as she trimmed off the remainder of my hair. He shook his head in disbelief.

'Ireland must be the luckiest place in the world to grow up,' he said. 'No wonder it took us hundreds of years to give the fucking place back to you.'

I lied to M later and told her that my new hairstyle – or rather the lack of one – was intentional. She barely commented, which in hindsight wasn't all that surprising since the average crew cut was hardly an anomaly for guys of army-going age. In the pub that night, I caught sight of my reflection in a mirror above the bartender's head. What a sight I was! I looked like a 1950s Irish teenager whose hair had been shaved to rid it of lice infestation.

Arthur, the English mechanic whom I'd met in the garage the previous week, was sitting at the end of the bar just inches away from the only draught beer dispenser in the pub, or indeed within fifty kilometres of the kibbutz. He informed me that he always sat on that particular stool. Its proximity to the beer tap was no accident. Following a long stint in the Merchant Navy, he told me, he and his wife had become a member of a pioneering group in the Negev. Eventually, they'd been absorbed into the kibbutz, and they now had two boys.

The kibbutzniks in general were made up of quite an eclectic bunch of people. Everyone was from somewhere else and had a great story to tell about how it was that they had ended up there. Most of them, their kids included, spoke at least two languages. Many of them spoke even more than two languages. For example, an Argentinian parent would speak Spanish only to their child but the child would reply in Hebrew, as it was the language of their school and their peers, Hebrew was, therefore, the children's first language. The same rule applied to parents of American, English, Russian, French, Australian or Dutch origin.

The following week, M and I made arrangements to meet in Beersheba for our 'dinner date'. The plan was that I would get the bus after work and that she, instead of coming home from school, would meet me in the local mall. The bus was quite full, but I managed to get a window seat. About ten minutes into the journey the bus stopped and picked up a middle-aged Bedouin Arab. He shuffled his way down the aisle and landed in beside me. He smelt as if he'd slept beside a campfire all night. Maybe he had.

In Beersheba, M gave me a tour of the mall, but it looked like a shopping centre you'd find anywhere in the world. It had one or two redeeming features, with air conditioning being at the top of the list. On the lower level, it had a cinema and a food court. McDonald's hadn't as yet invaded the Holy Land but they had their own equivalent – McDavid's. It was situated at the end of a large common eating area encircled by about ten differently styled restaurants. You could order anything from a

Chinese to a pizza to falafel to kebabs, and then sit anywhere you liked. I'd eaten doner kebabs before but nothing as good as the one I ate that day. I asked M if there was somewhere a little more authentic that we could go other than a shopping mall. There was a Bedouin open market, she said, a *shuk*, which was open for the afternoon. We left the mall, walking past the bus station and along the main road out of Beersheba. It was only a fifteen-minute walk, but not since my stint at the bus station in Tel Aviv had I felt just how far away from home I really was.

The cars whizzed by spraying up clouds of dust and sand into our faces, which only further burdened our breathing the already oxygen-starved air. I think there may actually be an Israeli law that requires drivers to blow their horns every time their car changes gear. Elsewhere, plastic bags and empty food packets clung to every kerb. I wondered if Dublin was cleaner due to the tenacity of its County Council road sweepers, or simply as a result of the almost constant flow of rainwater through the city's streets. The streets of Beersheba hadn't seen a drop of water in almost a year; this was evidently of little importance to the Bedouin who passed us, or indeed to his pet camel, which he was leading by a leash. Two hitchhiking darkly tanned soldiers, their M16s hanging loosely from their shoulders, turned and ogled M – or maybe they were ogling me.

The *shuk* itself was a cacophony of Arabic and Hebrew wails mixed with various animal brays. There were about a hundred stalls selling pots and pans, children's toys, music, cutlery, clothes and lots and lots of food. M bought some very sweet and dense pastries – a traditional Moroccan dessert – which her mother had learned how to make when she was growing up in Casablanca, in North Africa.

'Really?' I said. 'That's a coincidence. My mother was born in Cabra – in North Dublin.'

The following week, there was another holy day, *Yom Kippur*. It is one of the holiest days of the year but it fell on a Saturday so we volunteers felt a little cheated at not getting another day off. It was also a day of fasting, which thankfully wasn't obligatory. The kibbutz was already a fairly quiet place to

179

live in, especially on a Saturday, but there was an added stillness in the air that day.

Instead of going to the dining hall for lunch, Charlie fired up the barbeque and made us all cheeseburgers from some meat he'd 'liberated' from the kitchen. Throw on a few onions and open a beer and you've got the finest cheeseburgers in Israel – most likely the only cheeseburgers in Israel. Kosher food is complicated and there doesn't seem to be any succinct explanation to the intricacies of its customs and regulations, but obviously pork isn't allowed and meat and dairy never mix. I suppose then that it shouldn't have come as too much of a surprise to us when a kibbutznik on a pushbike stopped outside our rooms and asked us to put out the barbeque. We hadn't heard him approach as we had The Stones turned up loud. Two hundred people fasting and praying and all they could hear was 'Satisfaction' and all they could smell was juicy meat sizzling away.

The volunteers had a member of the kibbutz assigned to them, to act as a sort of liaison officer, someone, I suppose, that the kibbutz could register a complaint with if a volunteer was misbehaving, drinking too much or constantly being late for work, that sort of thing. We were lucky enough to have a kibbutznik called Eddie. He was originally from Sheffield and his mother, a judge, used to come and visit him. Years later he was kicked out of the kibbutz, but that's a story for another day.

A keen photographer, he had some great shots of the desert hanging on the walls of his house. He also had – and I hesitate to use the word fetish – an interest in photographing people naked and had a knack of persuading his subjects to strip. I particularly remember the shots of a stunningly beautiful girl called Asia, but there were many others, some of them volunteers.

One afternoon I saw him getting off the bus from Beersheba with a folder in his hand. He called me over and invited me back to his place to view his latest work – a German male volunteer, whose name I can't remember, posing naked in one of the orchards outside the kibbutz. The shots were mostly black and white, but some were sepia, and even I could appreciate the artistic nature of what he was trying to accomplish. Trees, desert, one-with-nature, nudity, one world etc – I get it. But I failed to understand however what purpose, artistic merit – or metaphor – his subject's erection allegedly represented. I began to wonder how Eddie had managed to create the desired effect surrounded, by only trees. Some things, I thought, are best left in the dark.

Eddie was the first kibbutznik I confided in about M and me. He was happy for me but warned me about it becoming common knowledge. If it did, I'd be thrown off the kibbutz very quickly, and it wouldn't make any difference whether M's mother disagreed or not.

'Tell you what,' he said to me. 'How about I take M out to the desert for a few nice photos?'

Much to Aengus's consternation, after about two weeks of working with Itai, I stopped checking the worksheet every evening. The harvesting season seemed to be winding to a close and, if the work was getting done, then I guess Rosa saw no reason to switch me. This would change later, however, as the volunteers were advised by their respective embassies to get out of Dodge.

Itai and I were becoming good friends. I suspected though that it was because my accent reminded him of the Irish girl, Marie, who'd broken his heart. I had made an incorrect assumption about their relationship, however. Apparently, things had been quite strong between them right up until the time she had left and gone back to Ireland. After that, she cut off all contact with him. He had tried countless times to reach her, but she never replied.

One afternoon, I was asked to fill in and take over the role of dishwasher for a couple of hours during lunchtime. I was playing my Hot House Flowers tape, and I waited until he was putting his dishes away. There was a sad love song called 'Sweet

Marie' playing. As soon as I saw him, I played it at full volume. He didn't even flinch when he heard it, didn't even acknowledge my 'bad joke', just left the dining room and went out and down the stairs. A couple of minutes later, just as the song was ending, a full bucket of cold water was emptied over my head. There wasn't an inch of me that wasn't soaked through. Itai placed the empty bucket on the ground beside me and walked away.

I was doubly punished the next day when I was given the job of cleaning out the gutters along the edge of the dining room roof. Later, Itai admitted that he never did it because he was afraid of heights. I can't imagine there are too many people in the world who are afraid of heights but manage to jump out of a plane for a living.

Around this time, there was a mass influx of Soviet Jews to Israel. Mikhail Gorbachev had opened up the emigration rules just as the United States had started to curb its immigration policy. The result was that Soviet Jews began to arrive in Israel in their tens of thousands. Over the next ten years, they would succeed in changing the physical and political landscape of the country. In the meantime, there were over four hundred caravan sites set up across the country to accommodate them, the biggest one being in Beersheba. On our kibbutz, a site was cleared near the volunteers' houses where about twenty caravans were installed in preparation for Russian families.

Itai used one of the empty caravans as a storeroom for his drum kit. After work, we'd head over there for a while, and he'd bash away while I smoked or just sat on the step looking out at the sun setting over the desert. Then I'd head back to my room, and either sit outside with someone drinking a beer or fall sleep for an hour or two. Afterwards, I'd eat supper with the rest of the guys in the dining room and meet M at about eight or nine, depending on her schedule.

While details may blur and fade away somewhat with the passage of time, the essence of an era never fades. I worked hard in an ostensibly menial job, slept on a wonky bed in a small room with two other people, had barely enough possessions to fill a duffle bag (most of them being old clothes), and I lived in a country which was on the brink of a major war. These are the details recalled with some effort, but the essence of that time was one of constant laughter and happiness. I'd spend the days laughing and joking with Itai under a glorious sun, and the evenings with the most beautiful girl I'd ever met. Things would change soon, but things always change. Without change, life becomes boring, stagnant and inevitable, and then what's the point of it all?

One evening M was late. I was waiting over half an hour for her to arrive (where else was I going to go?). As I waited, I began to make the mistake, and it's always a mistake, of second-guessing the future. If it all ended today, I thought, if the war came, and I had to go home, or if M just didn't turn up that night, or if the kibbutz found out about us and threw me out, where would this leave me? What would it all have been for?

Through the dark branches of the trees, a canopy of a million stars stared serenely down, and suddenly I felt apprehensive about the future. I felt as if I were basking in a warm swimming pool, and any thoughts of climbing out of the pool were merely a distraction from these moments of bliss. The evenings were getting cooler, and I was wearing my black jacket. The first breeze of winter caught me off guard, and I pulled up my collar to keep warm. As I reached into my jacket pocket for my cigarettes, I heard hurried footsteps coming along the road in my direction, and I slid the cigarettes back.

13

It was the last week in November and three significant events occurred within a few days of each other. The first was inevitable. M and I had become a bit bored hanging around the same spot and had started taking walks around the kibbutz at night, albeit on the darker streets. We were spending more and more time together, probably every evening at this stage. On the days when she worked in the kitchen, we'd sneak down to the bomb shelter at lunchtime. Occasionally, we'd be really brave and go for a walk in the desert in the afternoon. Her English was also improving, almost by the day – in fact so much so that her English teacher was curious to know if she was receiving private tutorials. In a way, I suppose she was.

One night though, it must have been around eleven o'clock, we were saying goodnight to each other, and what started out as a quick kiss ended up getting a little heavier and for a couple of minutes we forgot where we were. I got a sense we were being watched, and when I opened my eyes, I saw a figure standing and looking at us. M glanced over her shoulder. She practically pushed me away when she saw who it was. The woman turned and walked away.

'Oh shit, oh shit,' M keep saying.

'Who was that?' I asked.

'Chagit,' she said. 'She's in charge of the whole *Nurim.*'

Turns out that one of the last people we would have wanted to see us together had just seen us. There was nothing we could do. M said she'd speak to her mother about it, and we said goodnight.

The next event happened the following day on 29 November. On that day, the UN Security Council passed a resolution that gave Iraq until 15 January to withdraw from

Kuwait and it authorised member states to then use 'all necessary means' to force Iraq to withdraw. There were rumours that there were already tens of thousands of US troops being prepared for departure to the Gulf region. Looking back on it now, in a way, the second event cancelled out the first. Impending war has a way of taking the edge off otherwise important problems and moral issues. Whether Chagit said anything or not I don't know, but as the prospect of war got closer, and M and I got closer, she and I started to further test the boundaries of our self-imposed limitations.

The following Friday morning I heard rumours about a mini-volunteer trip. Most kibbutzim have a policy of bringing their volunteers on a road trip every few months, at the kibbutz's expense of course. A few volunteers had already left, and they weren't being replaced. The number of volunteers coming to Israel had, understandably, diminished significantly and would soon cease completely. Eddie confirmed the rumour at lunchtime. A day trip was planned for the following day; it would take in Masada and the Dead Sea. We were like children who'd been told they were being taken to Disneyland. Most of us even left the pub early that Friday night in order to get a half-decent night's sleep; the chartered bus, we were told, was leaving at 9am and whoever wasn't ready at that time wouldn't be going anywhere.

I considered not going as I figured that with all the volunteers out of the way, M and I would have the place to ourselves. But M said I'd enjoy it and insisted that I go. Aengus, who'd stayed on in the pub after we'd left, was nowhere to be seen the next morning. He hadn't slept in his bed the previous night either. Just when Eddie had decided we couldn't wait any longer, Chad called out from the back of the bus to wait. Everyone cheered and whistled as Aengus came running, with Jenny five paces behind him. No questions needed to be asked; her meek expression as she slid into her seat and Aengus's beaming smile said it all. Everyone was in good spirits and gave a big cheer as we drove out the kibbutz gates. We were an easily pleased bunch.

Instead of heading for Beersheba, we followed a narrower route through the desert. The road twisted and turned, rising and falling as if it had been simply constructed on top of sand dunes. We passed Yeruham, a development town built in the 1950s. It seemed, however, as if little development had taken place in the intervening years. We continued on until we reached a larger town called Dimona before joining a wider road to the east.

Dimona is a settlement town for a sect known as the Black Hebrews. They had moved to Israel from the United States in 1969 under the Law of Return. As of yet however they had not been granted any official status in Israel. The sect believes themselves to be descended from the ten lost tribes of Israel; they have even gone so far as to claim that they are the only true descendents of the ancient Israelites. They have their own customary way of life. Polygamy is allowed, birth control is forbidden, and they follow their own dietary laws which are similar to a vegan-type diet.

The desert lay open for miles around us until just past Dimona, where high fences festooned with large red and yellow warning signs, ran parallel to the road. Eddie informed us that this was Israel's Nuclear Research Centre. Ambiguity still prevails today in the international community as to whether this site is used for the production of nuclear weapons, but Eddie confirmed for us that day that it was true. You just can't trust anyone from Sheffield to keep a secret.

We drove over several mounds in the road, which Eddie told us in Hebrew are called 'Irish bridges'. These are slightly raised sections of road which are susceptible to flooding during the rainy season; the 'Irish bridges' allow the rain water to flow over them. I can only imagine that they were named thus by some British army engineer with a wicked sense of humour.

We continued on for almost an hour until we started our descent. Down and down we went, our driver using the engine as a break, while on the opposite side of the road buses and cars spluttered and struggled in their effort to climb the steep incline. About half way down the mountain we passed a sign that read 'Sea Level'. When we finally got to Masada and got off the bus, it was a lot hotter than it had been at the kibbutz. The date was 1 December. I couldn't begin to imagine how hot this place must get in July and August.

We climbed Masada, and Eddie gave us a brief tour of the place; the Romans, the siege; the mass suicide. Just as in Ireland and around the world, the sacred and revered sites seemed to be based on events where things went horribly wrong. More often than not, our heroes and admired historical figures are martyrs – great people who were killed or who struggled ceaselessly to the bitter end. The view stretched out across the Dead Sea with its white-encrusted salty shores, and onwards to the distant mountains of Jordan. Today, the army uses Masada at night for torch-lit 'falling-out' parades and ceremonies. Military-might; enemies below; a people oppressed. Roles and costumes have changed, but the stage remains indistinguishable and indifferent. Even from that high up and on such a clear day, I failed to see the point of it all.

In, or rather on, the Dead Sea, Charlie and I floated out a little too far, and reached the centre which marks the border between Israel and Jordan. A Jordanian plane swooped down and flew over our heads. I've been back to the Dead Sea since then, and they now have special swimming areas sectioned off to prevent people from swimming out too far. I'm quite sure we weren't the only ones to unwittingly cross into Jordan with only our swimming shorts as ID, but I'd like to think that we played at least some small part in the diplomatic relations of the two countries. We showered the sliminess of the salty sea off our skin and then drove to the small strip of hotels and cafes along the coast. We ate shawarma and drank ice-cold Goldstar in the shade while listening to the cafe owner's music. The singer's voice filled the cafe as we all ate in silence. She sang a beautiful lament, which in the sun, sounded like rain. It made me think of M and it reminded me that one day I would have to go home, and that all of this and perhaps even M herself would become little more than a dream. I suddenly felt desperate to get back to see her, and, for the first time during many times in my life, I felt both joy and sadness simultaneously. Two emotions sharing the same vein; two trains running along the same track. I still hadn't any plans to leave Israel, but there was a definite sense of the changing of a season; a grey ominous cloud on the horizon of a perfectly blue sky. I asked the cafe owner for the name of the singer and he wrote it down for me – Etti Ankri. At the very least, I figured, I'd have the music to remind me of this time, a sort of musical memento – a proof that this happiness was once real.

The sun had started its decent behind us, and we watched the colours of the Jordanian mountains as they changed from browns to golds to purples. We might still be sitting there today were it not for our bus driver who pulled up alongside where we were seated and blasted the horn repeatedly.

The third significant event occurred when Itai opened his post the following day, Sunday. He and his platoon were being summoned back to the army two months before their due date. He had one week left on the kibbutz.

I wish I could say that my first concerns were for his safety, but, sadly, I thought of matters more important to my own heart – who was going to be the next hatzran? I wanted to ask Itai if he thought they'd ask me to assume this role, but he kept moaning about returning to the army. If he would just give it a rest for five minutes, I thought, perhaps I could turn the conversation towards the hatzran position, but he was relentless in his complaining. I thought it rather selfish of him.

At lunchtime, I saw him go over to Rosa and show her his letter. They chatted for a few minutes, and then he came back to the table.

'Rosa says I've got to show you everything, that you'll be the hatzran from next week,' he said.

I tried to contain my delight at the news. I didn't want to appear too insensitive to Itai's gloominess, so I tried to play it cool.

'I'll meet you downstairs,' I told him and went into the kitchen.

Charlie was, of course, happy for me but then Aengus came in and broke the news that he was heading home in two weeks' time. He wanted, he said, to be home for Christmas and then look for a job in the New Year. I could tell that Charlie was a bit put out by this. Despite their constant piss taking, they'd also shared a lot of laughs. Believe it or not, the following year they ended up travelling to the Far East together.

That afternoon I bought a little black notebook from the colbo and then spent the next week following Itai around and writing everything down. I was determined to take this position seriously. He carried around with him a set of keys that would make a jailer at San Quentin feel inferior. As far as I could tell, he had the key for pretty much every door and lock in the kibbutz.

The hatzran position is basically a yard man-cum-maintenance man. The word '*hatzer*' means 'yard'. My job involved the general upkeep of the kibbutz, which included some small plumbing jobs such as the unblocking of toilets and sinks. This part of the job I already knew about and it even gave me a certain satisfaction to unblock a toilet and allow all the – literally – crap to run free. It was far from poetic by any stretch of the imagination, but there was definitely a certain personal and mentally idyllic release that always followed a particularly gruesome blockage.

However, even though I'd been working with Itai on and off for the preceding couple of months, new responsibilities that I had previously been unaware of began to emerge. Some of these responsibilities were a little unpleasant. I'm not saying that Itai never took on these responsibilities. Far be it for me to cast any false aspersions on my hatzran mentor. All I'm saying is that he never did them whenever I was around.

For example, I had no idea that the hatzran was responsible for the fly population – or rather depopulation – on the kibbutz. Flies in Israel are not like your common-or-garden flies in Ireland. They're bigger and tougher and faster. When one lands on your skin you can really feel it. I've no doubt whatsoever that if I had ever wrestled one of those little buggers to the ground, I'd have found gangland tattoos on at least one of their six legs. This type of contrast was quite common in the case of a lot of things in Israel. Everything appeared the same as everywhere else – only a little bit tougher, a little bit more resilient. I'm not romanticising when I say that even Israeli grass isn't as soft as the grass in Ireland. Israeli grass blades are wide and hard. Perhaps everything – even the people – has to be a little tougher because of the harsh living conditions.

For such bothersome and gruesome little creatures, the Hebrew word for flies is a rather cute word – '*zvoovim*'. Their overpopulation was kept at bay by about twenty flytraps, which were hung arbitrarily throughout the kibbutz. They were beehive-shaped objects and made of clear plastic. Once Itai had shown me an example of one, I began to see them everywhere – mostly hanging from trees or close to the bins. Taking them down and emptying out the hundreds or perhaps thousands of dead flies wasn't the worst of it. The really repulsive part was the bait. A more rancid and just plain nasty smell, I had never experienced either before or since. The base of the trap was filled with this concoction, and whatever the hell it was, the flies adored it. Maybe one day I will have to answer for my war crimes of genocide against the fly population, but I will recite as thousands have done before me – I was only doing my job.

Another new job that miraculously materialised that week was the cleaning of the main sewer. Basically, everything that was flushed down a toilet had to go through this metal grate near the outer perimeter fence. Of course, anything larger than – well, let's not get too barbaric here – anything too large would get stuck between the iron grids. I would then, using an industrial-sized hose, unclog the grate, thus ensuring that all passageways (of all kinds) were kept free-flowing and happy.

If I failed to clear it out at least once a week, or if there was a large celebration on the kibbutz, and the sewer was overworked, then the grate would become blocked and an ear-piercing siren would ring. This happened to me on more than one occasion. Leaving a party quite drunk one night and then looking down into a thirty-foot hole full of fresh sewage, while I fired a stream of high-pressure water into it was, in hindsight, not the smartest of things to do. I can't imagine it would have been a very pleasant death if I had lost my footing, but at least the surviving flies would have had the last laugh as my tight-lipped face went slowly under. I doubt that I would have opened my mouth, even to scream for help.

My relationship with M came to a bit of a crossroads when rumours and whispers of our affair reached all the way to her parents' table in the dining room. I really didn't care what people said, unless it meant that M and I would end up not being able to see each other. I was also aware that her mother already knew, and we'd even exchanged the odd conspiratorial nod in each other's direction. Something that I was afraid of though was that a slur might be cast on M's family, or that her brothers would get a bit of slagging about the situation. It was all very well for me not to give a shit about gossip and innuendo, but everyone else involved had to live here.

Another factor that intimidated me was her father. He wore a firm and grave expression barely hidden behind a heavy black beard. He worked as a pathologist in the hospital in Beersheba, so I was acutely aware that the disposal of my body wouldn't prove too great of a challenge for him. Eventually, however, her parents had no option but to respond in some way to all the gossip. Rather than forbid M from seeing me or getting Eddie to have a word with me or just getting me thrown off the kibbutz that day, they decided to do what, I believe, only they of all the families on the kibbutz would have done – they invited me for dinner in their home.

I had quite a good reputation on the kibbutz at this stage, but I was under no illusions that one word from M's parents, and I'd be on the next bus. Looking back now, I'm convinced that any other parents would have done just that. Although both were born in Morocco they had a French upbringing, and who better in the world to understand affairs of the heart than the French?

They had an amazing command of English for people who had never lived in an English-speaking country and this helped enormously. French was the language of the house, and although my own grasp of French wasn't sufficient to enable me to converse with any great fluency, it helped a bit. M's mother was an artist and the house had a bohemian but organised feel to it. Interestingly though, I learned years later that for generations every girl born into the family, on her mother's side, ended up moving abroad and subsequently living in a different country from the one in which they were born. So, I suppose that certain inevitability – albeit unwanted – had already been anticipated, accepted and even assumed.

M's father turned out to be a benign if somewhat stoic individual. I found his austere reputation unwarranted. He was profoundly respected throughout the kibbutz, which I'm sure he quite relished and even enjoyed. Perhaps he felt that displaying anything other than a sombre and sober disposition would cost him the reverence that was afforded to him by his peers. Secretly, he loved dirty jokes, especially if they related to medicine or religion.

I remember little of the actual dinner except that it was quite formal but pleasant. After the meal, just as we were saying our goodbyes, M offered, in front of everyone, to walk me back to my room. We left the house together and turned right along the main road through the kibbutz. As natural as plucking a wild flower, I took her hand in mine. From that day on, we openly walked together, talked together and even sat together in the dining room. The gossiping ended, and, amazingly, even the world, quite indifferently, continued to turn.

Before he left, Itai gave me a crash course, metaphorically speaking, on the ins and outs of driving the tractor and all the other work vehicles which were now at my disposal. I was happy to take over the role of hatzran, but I was also, of course, sad to see Itai go. I would miss him both as a work colleague and as a friend. Before departing he presented me with his red army beret, which I still have today.

On my first morning as I mounted the tractor, the ridiculously large bunch of keys now hanging from my side, I felt as if I'd become lord and master of the whole damn kibbutz. This conceited belief was quickly dissipated by a cock-up on my very first day. I like to put it down to my being a little over-zealous, it being my first week and all that. I was keen to make a good first impression so I started off by driving around the kibbutz and collecting all the rubbish from the skips. If I found something that wasn't tied down, I hauled it off. Near a cornered-off area at the back of the factory where all the waste product was kept, I loaded up several boxes and dumped them in the trench in the desert. Generally there's often a bit of tidying up done by the kibbutz members on their only day off, Saturday, so any tree cuttings or bush debris were always left by the side of the road for me to collect. By the end of the day, the trench was full to the brim, so I decided to burn it all before finishing up.

I was pretty wrecked after my day, and at about four in the afternoon, I decided to go to sleep for an hour or two. I was about to get into bed when Charlie came in.

'How'd your first day go?' he asked.

'Great,' I said. 'Not as much craic without Itai, but it was good.'

'It'll probably take you a few days to find your feet,' he advised and started to make a cup of tea. He bent down and looked out of the window in the kitchen as he filled the kettle. 'Jesus, that smoke just seems to be getting worse doesn't it?'

'The what?' I asked.

'The smoke.'

'What smoke?'

'What smoke?' he asked. 'How could you not have seen that big dirty black cloud over the desert?'

I ran outside and saw, just as Charlie had described, an enormous black stream of smoke travelling across the sky towards the Kfar. I looked at its source and estimated that it was coming from the trench where I'd burnt all the rubbish. My heart sank. I got dressed and drove out in my tractor, but there were already a few people there. The smoke was pumping out of the hole and was showing no signs of letting up. Complaints and phone calls were made from the Kfar, but there was little that anyone could do to stop it. It turned out that I'd thrown in some boxes filled with a glue waste product. The boxes were supposed to have been collected by a recycling company. God only knows how much ozone I managed to burn off that day.

There was one other responsibility of the hatzran that I was aware of, but had chosen to forget about until absolutely necessary. Often, people from outside the kibbutz would drive in, and rather than drop off their kittens and puppies at a dog pound, they'd leave them at the bus stop, possibly hoping that one of the kibbutz members would adopt them. Obviously, it was not possible to allow stray animals to wander about the place unhindered, so it was the task of the hatzran to, well, dispose of them.

One day, I was driving by the bus stop on the Manitou, the large diesel forklifts, and had a skip attached to the forks. One of the kibbutz members, Eli, called me over and showed me a cardboard box containing five dark-haired puppies that someone had abandoned. I told him to leave them in the box and to put the box on top of the skip; that I'd take them out to the desert for now, and then have someone else 'take care' of them later. I drove off, the puppies yelping at the excitement of this new adventure of theirs. They were enjoying the rush of cool air and I was smiling at them when I hit the first speed bump. The box was catapulted about a foot into the air, and for a moment all five puppies were suspended in midair, their tiny legs sprawled out in front of them. Two were lucky enough to fall back down into the skip. A third dropped between the small front wheel and the huge rear wheel on my right. I slammed on the brakes, but a few seconds later his little body emerged on the other side of the rear wheel – an indistinguishable representation of its former self. In hindsight, this puppy was actually one of the lucky ones.

The fourth puppy landed on the other side of the road and broke its leg. I picked him up and placed him gently inside the box with the rest of his clan. Leaving the engine of the Manitou idling, I searched between the olive trees for the fifth puppy but I couldn't find it.

Out in the desert, I placed the cardboard box on top of the three remaining puppies. The kibbutz protocol was to administer a quick whack on the head with the back of a shovel, but I always preferred if a bullet were used, so I set off to find Arthur. He jumped onto the side of the Manitou with his rifle slung over his shoulder, and we drove back out into the desert. The puppies all yelped enthusiastically when I removed the cardboard box. Arthur looked a little ridiculous as he pointed the long barrel of the rifle at the first puppy's head and took aim. A quick punch of noise into the air and the puppy dropped dead as quickly as if someone had turned off an electrical switch. The second one mustn't have been the smartest chap in the class as he started to trot happily towards Arthur as if saying 'me next.' Arthur obliged. The third one was a bit sharper and started to edge away as quickly as possible. Unfortunately, due to his broken leg his efforts had little effect. He managed to move fast enough though, as Arthur had to follow his progress through the sight of his rifle, and then BANG.

I drove around the kibbutz for fifteen minutes or so with Arthur riding shotgun, literally, looking for the fifth puppy. If we had actually managed to find it, I'm not sure whether Arthur would have just shot at it from the side of the Manitou. If it survived somehow, somewhere, I hope it had a half decent life. Enough life anyway to make up for the rest of his family who we slaughtered that morning.

September turned out to have been a great month to choose to arrive at the kibbutz, as it seemed that no more than two weeks went by without some religious festivity or other taking place, resulting in us being given at the very least a day off. About half way through December we had Hanukkah. I'd never even heard of any of these holidays, so it was all new to me. Since then, I've celebrated these holidays many times, but I'm still not too sure what they're supposed to represent. But then again, I've no idea why I put a fir tree in my sitting room at Christmas, or what on earth bunny rabbits have to do with the resurrection of Christ at Easter. Hanukkah has something to do with oil miraculously staying alight for eight days, and during Hanukah, a menorah candle is lit every day. But, just like Christmas, Hanukkah mostly just means giving and receiving gifts, but with the additional rather bizarre practice of doughnuts thrown in.

Now that everything was out in the open, M and I got to see each other all the time - especially now that I was hatzran and didn't really have a boss as such. If she was working in the kitchen, I'd always manage to find some urgent work to do in that area and we'd sneak off on our own for a while. Often, we'd take the bus into Beersheba and either get something to eat or go to a movie. Unlike cinemas back home, Israeli cinemas would have an interval during the movie. At seemingly any point during the film, even while one of the main characters was in the middle of a sentence, or during some crucial turning point in the story, the screen would shut down, and the house lights would come on. The audience would clamber out for more popcorn and drinks and then, after an apparently arbitrary period of time, the movie would start up again; the sound and picture bursting back onto the screen exactly where they had left off. Most times, the cinema management remembered, after a minute or so, to turn the house lights off again. When nearing the end of a movie, and in preparation for the cinema audience's departure, the usher would obligingly open the exit door near the bottom corner of the screen, which succeeded in enveloping much of the screen in distracting light from the hall below. If the movie in the adjoining cinema ended before our one did, that audience would begin filing noisily past the open door and some of the audience would inevitably pop in to catch the end of our movie.

If there was nothing special going on, I'd head over to her parents' house and we'd hang out there. If she hadn't yet arrived home, I'd get some basic Hebrew lessons from her mother while I waited. They played some nice music in that house – classic performers like Ray Charles, Louis Armstrong and Ella Fitzgerald. They also introduced me to other French language singers like Yves Duteil and Jacques Brel. They sort of adopted me in a way, and I was very grateful for their generosity towards me. My standard of living certainly improved considerably from then on.

Sometimes M and I would just go to her room, and while she was working on a project at her desk, I'd lie on her bed and read, with Sting or Seal playing in the background. I'd catch the crumbs of conversations as people walked by her window – Hebrew, Spanish, Russian, and even English, with the elasticity of its varying accents – a modern day city of Babylon. On the window of her bedroom were Venetian blinds through which the evening light would fall on her face; sometimes, instead of reading, I'd just watch her. In the corner of her room was a deep orange-coloured lamp, shaped like a large heart. As the evenings drew closer and the days shortened, the lamp would grow brighter and brighter, until you almost felt as if it would just burst with the heat of it all.

On Christmas Day, Charlie and I, fair-weather Christians that we were, took full advantage of our entitlement to a day off. The volunteer numbers were diminishing rapidly, as the UN Security Council deadline of 15 January approached. There were no new volunteers arriving, which meant that we could have taken advantage of the situation and got ourselves separate rooms, but we stayed sharing for the time being.

Anyway, now that Aengus had left, the room seemed to have doubled in size. That year's Christmas Day was certainly the strangest I've ever experienced. While the entire of Ireland awoke to a day marked by giving and receiving gifts, excited kids, great big dinners and RTÉ One showing *It's a Wonderful Life*, Charlie and I woke to a Tuesday. The pair of us sauntered around the kibbutz enjoying the Christmas sunshine, and in the afternoon I called home. I'd already told the family about M, although I'd lied about her age.

Another week went by, and after the New Year's celebrations, which we spent in the pub, a few more volunteers departed until the only ones remaining were Charlie, Guy and me. This situation forced us to make more of an effort to mix with the kibbutz members, and we made some great friends among them. By now, it was quite cold at night, and my nose would go red from the chill in the air as we smoked outdoors. My cigarette intake had increased to two packs a day. Charlie's fan had been replaced with a small electrical heater, which we used to make toast in the evenings. Although we were told not to do so, we'd often leave its burning red glow illuminating the room while we slept – it was so cold there at night.

There was very much an atmosphere of a people in waiting throughout this period. Mostly unspoken though. It certainly wasn't Israel's first time to be placed under threat, but the perpetual sense of foreboding was quite tangible nonetheless. One day, I was working somewhere or other and listening to a Sinead O'Connor song – the one with a line that goes, 'Listen to the man in the liquor store, Yelling "anybody want a drink before the war?",' and Amit was walking by, and he called over, 'I'll have a scotch please,' and kept walking.

Eventually though, our waiting came to an end.

14

It was at some ungodly hour on a Saturday morning when the first air raid siren went off.

Apparently, the general procedure whenever there was a prospect of war breaking out was to clear out the kibbutz's several underground bomb shelters and to stock them with whatever supplies were necessary in order to cater for the families in that area. This war was different however, in that for the first time the use of chemical weapons was a real possibility. So, instead of running to the nearest bomb shelter, Israeli families were advised to select a room in their homes and to seal its windows from the outside using adhesive tape. Once everyone was inside the room, the door was then sealed from the inside.

The volunteers had selected one of the empty chalet rooms and had already sealed up the windows in preparation for the weapons attack. A couple of months before Operation Desert Storm had begun on 17 January, gas masks had been distributed throughout the country; it was forbidden to travel anywhere without them. Apart from the gas masks, we were also given syringes filled with Atropine which was to be self-administered as an antidote to God only knows what. One sharp swift jab into the leg was apparently enough to do the trick. Charlie and I were prepared to wait until bodies began collapsing around us before we would stab ourselves in the leg with a hypodermic syringe.

Around the period when Operation Desert Storm was little more than a few etchings on the back of George Bush's dinner napkin, the Israeli Government decreed that its citizens were to seal themselves into a room. The residents of Kibbutz Sederah thought that all their Christmases – or rather all their

Hanukkahs – had come at once. The reason was that at the time there were very few factories anywhere producing the high-grade tape required to make a room airtight. Sederah had one of those factories. It worked non stop for quite a few months to meet the demand for the tape. So much so in fact that while countries and populations were rebuilding their lives after the Gulf War, Kibbutz Sederah treated all two hundred of its members to a long weekend at a hotel at the seaside resort of Eilat. I'm quite sure that the manufacturers of the Gulf War gas masks, bullets, patriot missiles and other military hardware involved didn't fare too badly either.

The bombing of Iraq began the night before Israel was bombed. My family in Dublin was naturally quite worried at this stage. It's always harder when you're geographically removed from a particular situation. Subsequently, my mother told me that the family dog started barking early on that Saturday morning, and that when she went downstairs to investigate the reasons for his barking, she had switched the television on to find that Tel Aviv was being bombed. Almost nobody had mobile phones in those days and, besides, we were sealed into our little room with our gas masks at the ready. After a couple of hours the air raid sirens wailed again indicating the all clear. The Israeli government and then the international media announced that there were no chemical weapons attached to the scuds, so we unsealed the door, and emerged to see the sun rising over the desert, and my mother, in Dublin, went back to bed.

Those first few days of the Gulf War were strange. Nobody really knew what to do. Most of us tried to carry on as normal, but at night the air raid sirens would begin wailing and people would head to their sealed rooms and try to get some sleep. After only a couple of nights, Charlie and I started using the adhesive tape to block out the noise in our room that was coming from the sirens and just stayed in bed.

One evening, as I was eating alone at the volunteers' table in the dining room, the sirens went off. I had just started my salad and I could see absolutely no need to leave the dining room. Other people did get up and leave, however, and it was only when the manager of the dining room started to turn off the lights that I budged. All of the streetlights had turned off automatically when the alarm was raised, so I walked back to my room in relative darkness.

There was an army practice range on one of the hills just beside the kibbutz. You could often hear gunfire on any given night of the week. They were practising that night, and as the siren wailed, it was interspersed by the sound of automatic gunfire echoing in the darkness through the hills. As pathetic as it may sound, that was probably as close as I ever got to experiencing what a war situation is like.

More importantly for me, the war was seriously curtailing opportunities for M and I to see one another. Her parents were understandably a little overprotective; they wanted her at home as often as possible in case the alarm was raised. I missed her terribly, but I wasn't about to go back to my room every evening and sit there waiting for the scuds to arrive. I started to work late into the evening, usually until it got dark, and I got friendly with some Russians, one in particular by the name of Alex. Occasionally, my European outlook on life would clash with the Israeli point of view, but often I found the Russians' way of thinking closer to my own.

It was also very easy, at first anyway, to take offence, from the kibbutzniks at rudimentary translations from Hebrew to English. Hebrew can be a very direct and commanding language and is often imbued with a bluntness that can be perceived as nothing short of rude. When an Israeli asks for someone to pass them the salt at a table, a direct translation, and the phrase most commonly used, is 'give me salt'. Similarly, I have been told, in a tone reserved for that of a recalcitrant mongrel, to 'wait', 'come', 'take', and to 'go'. Perhaps the etymology of the language stems from military roots and therefore has an inherent commanding or instructional foundation, but either way it took a little getting used to.

Sometimes in the afternoon, during the Gulf War, the newly arrived Soviet Jews would invite me to drink with them in their caravan. We would sit around a table and Alex, who spoke Russian, English, Spanish and Hebrew, would translate the conversation as best he could. There would be several bottles of vodka on the table and a few bottles of various types of juice. Apparently, Russians don't mix juice with vodka, which is what I was used to doing.

Each of us would have two glasses in front of us. Into the first was poured a generous measure of vodka which filled about a third of the glass. Their brand of vodka had a much harsher aroma than what I was used to. Into the other glass was poured the juice, almost to the brim. They would chat for a while, and then in unison they'd raise the glass of vodka and swallow it in one shot. The glass of juice was raised in the left hand before the empty vodka glass in the right hand was replaced on the table. In another swift motion, the juice was downed and the conversation continued.

The first time I drank vodka this way, I prepared myself to instantly vomit the vodka. However, once the juice followed quickly on the trail of the vodka, the vodka not only stayed down, but I could barely even taste it. I'd have several of these rounds with the Russians, then it'd be *Dasvidaniya* comrades and I'd leave. It was always the same though. I'd walk out quite sober, but as soon as I'd gone a few paces from the caravan and my lungs had filled with oxygen, it'd be like someone had whacked me on my skull with a hammer. I'd practically crawl for the remaining few hundred yards back to my room and collapse onto the bed.

Another afternoon, late in January, I befriended an American on the kibbutz, and we came up with the idea of driving to Tel Aviv to watch the scud missiles falling. In Tel Aviv, we met some American troops on the streets and stayed with them for a while, but as soon as the 'so what part of Texas are you from?' conversation petered out, we left. No scuds fell that night, and we headed home, driving by the patriot missile launchers on the off-chance that one might be fired.

The more the war continued on, the more apparent it became to me how small a threat the scuds actually posed. They were almost as inaccurate and as unpredictable as the patriot missiles that were supposed to be protecting us. Operation Desert Storm became more and more like a computer programme merely running in the background. Around the middle of February, however, our complacency was tested a little when the Iraqis fired three missiles at the nearby Dimona Nuclear Base. Because the incident happened in the middle of the night, I didn't get to see the missiles falling.

Towards the end of January it was time for Charlie to leave. The kibbutz community differed from most communities in the world in that there was forever a continuous turnover of people. Many would come for long periods, whether they were soldiers, volunteers, casual workers or even members, and then one day they'd be gone. We had so many 'going away' parties that at one point, it seemed that every other day somebody was leaving. We would live, work, eat, sleep with each other, share secrets, tell stories, weep, and of course laugh, fight, get drunk, open up about ourselves, and then, inevitably, have to say goodbye. I shared so much with these people that many of the attitudes and beliefs that I have today stem from that period. I have never met nor spoken to any of them since. I'm sure that for those who lived on the kibbutz, it taught invaluable life lessons of loss and departure that we all must face some day, but many times, for me anyway, they were hard-learned lessons.

When a volunteer initially arrives to Israel, they are given a three-month visa, which is stamped on their passport. This can be extended only once for a further three months. I was, of course, very sad to see Charlie leave, but just like at a funeral where tears are often shed in response to tangible reminders of our own mortality, I was reminded that my time to depart was fast approaching. It seemed as if talk of months had turned to weeks. M and I never mentioned it but the fact that I would be leaving in March was forever present. I'm sure there are many situations in people's lives that you believe that if you don't talk or think about them, then they may simply go away. Of course, they never do.

One morning in February, I was driving the tractor through the kibbutz when an F-16 flew right over me. It didn't appear to be going too fast, and it didn't even make any sound, but the moment it was out of sight my tractor shook from the explosion of noise and the vibrations it created in its wake. There was an air force base about twenty miles from Sederah. By the time the pilots were flying over the skies of the kibbutz, they had reached the speed of sound, and a large bang rang out in the sky, as the sound barrier was broken. Once, I was asleep in my apartment, when I felt as if the whole building had been lifted ten feet into the air and crashed back down again. I thought it was an earthquake and ran outside to see two F-16s flying away, low across the desert. I believe that complaints were regularly made to the base at the time.

As I didn't have much access, if any, to a television while I was on the kibbutz, I didn't experience the Gulf War in the way many of my friends and families did. Live coverage from CNN and Sky News seemed to have kept people informed and somewhat entertained late into the night. I do know though that on 24 February 1991 the ground forces moved into Iraq. I later saw some of the pictures of the Highway of Death, a six-lane highway between Iraq and Kuwait. A couple of days later, the retreating Iraqi troops were attacked at night along this road, and it was those pictures that helped George Bush to decide to end the war after only one hundred hours of sending in ground troops.

About a week before I was due to leave, Rosa, the Argentinian lady in charge of the work schedule, called me to her office after work, She gave me a beautifully wrapped box as a going away present, and when I opened it found a silver Cross pen. I looked along the side and it said 'Made in Ireland'.

Outside I bumped into one of the younger kids I'd become friendly with. I think they liked to practise their English on me.

He told me he had just seen a great movie called 'The Quiet Sheep'. I told him I'd never heard of it, but I would look out for it. It was only after he cycled away that I realised he had given me the direct translation of the movie *Silence of the Lambs*.

One late afternoon in January, I was sitting outside my place on my own having a cigarette. The volunteers' houses were a lot quieter than they had been when I first arrived. A Phil Collins' album was playing in my room, and the music poured out through the open window. The atmosphere was unusually humid and heavy. A track titled 'The Roof is Leaking' came on. At the end of the track there's a big instrumental build-up and, just as it started, I saw something that I hadn't seen for almost eight months – rain. A few drops at first, as if the clouds were being gently squeezed. Big drops bounced off the path beside me, as if thrown down from the heavens in large handfuls. Then heavier, like a dog shaking off water from its coat. The smell of moist dust filled the air. The smell of the switching of seasons. A smell of conclusion and change. The rain gained strength slowly, as the desert sand jumped up into the air to greet it, dancing for joy. I sat watching the rain and listened to the music, my cigarette extinguished in my hand. Then I wiped my face dry and went back inside.

Our selection of music was a little limited in the kibbutz. Whatever artist or group that a new volunteer brought with them was happily added to our mixed bag miscellany of music. There were many songs then that I remember. A sort of soundtrack for that time, I suppose. Like most couples, M and I had our own songs too. Perhaps ours were a little sadder and more unusual than most though. Jacques Brel – 'Ne me quitte pas' or Etti Ankri (the singer from the cafe at the Dead Sea) 'Roa Lecha Baenim'. It seems that the Jewish culture has as many songs of oppression and sadness as the Irish culture does. M and I took full advantage of those songs to express our own feelings of despondent departure.

On those final few days, I was very much overcome with a sense of leaving home.

Another little holiday, Tu Bishvat, popped up in the calendar at the beginning of February. This holiday revolves around the planting of trees in designated areas throughout Israel. This particular year, on our kibbutz, the barren ground surrounding the caravans was chosen as the selected area. The entire kibbutz community appeared after breakfast on a beautiful Saturday morning and helped with the planting. It was a typical kibbutz celebration – the old and the young playing and working together, the serving of food and drink, music playing, everyone chatting and laughing in the winter sunshine.

M and I were sitting together on a bench when I heard a camera go CLICK. Eddie stuck his head out from behind his lens and gave us a cheesy grin. A few days later, I found the photo he'd taken in my post box. I was wearing a red V-neck sweater with a white T-shirt underneath. M was wearing a white Aran sweater. The sky was the definition of blue. We looked so happy, and yet so blissfully unaware of our happiness. I don't know what particular activity or scene I was observing; all I know is that I was smiling and squinting slightly at the sun. M, sitting on my left, was also smiling and staring up at me with a melancholic devotion. I still have the photo, but today M's sweater has faded to a faint yellow, and the intensity of the sky colour has mellowed somewhat with the passage of time. Our expressions of contentment, optimism and rapture, however, have not.

As I sat on the plane leaving Tel Aviv a few weeks later, I held a book in my hand, that same photo pressed between the book's pages. I took it out and looked at it every few minutes, like a drowning man continuing to come up for air. My journey back to her had already begun. My thoughts reached out to capture any dreams of us being together again, any visions of our imagined life one day in the future – anything to suppress the very real thought and the possibility that I might never see her again.

I wished I was back in the kibbutz. I wished I was back with M. With my M. To bask again in the desert heat and in her love. To walk barefoot across the watered lawns of the kibbutz holding her hand. To sit beside her on the desert hill, where the sun would set as if it was setting for us and us alone. To lie on her bed under the red glow of her lamp; to watch her read, her lips moving softly as if kissing each word on the page.

Over a decade would pass before the day arrived when those dreams would become a reality. The journey I took to that day, and to that moment in the future, unfolded in wonder before me, unravelling beyond even my own imagination...

ABOUT THE AUTHOR

During the past two decades of repeated and extended visits abroad, a dichotomy of misspent youth and misspent dollars, the island of Ireland has watched, like the spectator of a tennis match, as Joseph Birchall ebbed and flowed his way between a Californian coast and an Israeli desert.

Now in his forties (early forties), the vagaries of youth have been evaporated, presumably by his sun chasing travels, and Joseph has pitched his tent and finally found a happy home, albeit only a stone's throw away from where he was born.

He now divides his time between… well, pretty much the same way everyone else does, except lately he's developed somewhat of an inexplicable aversion to chicken soup and an insatiable penchant for green olives.

He reminisces too much, but has stopped smoking, and is happy with this trade-off.

Thank you for reading this book. If you would like to contact Joseph for any reason, then you can find him at…

On Twitter - @anyjoesoap

Email: josephbirchall@mail.com

Printed in Great Britain
by Amazon

46317003R00128